Accelerated
Learning Programs

Accelerated
Learning Programs

ROBERT F. DeHAAN

Chairman, Department of Psychology
Hope College

1963
The Center for Applied Research in Education, Inc.
Washington, D.C.

St. Mary's College Library
Winona, Minnesota

Foreword

Dr. Robert DeHaan is remarkably well-qualified to write about the education of gifted children. He worked in one of the pioneer programs for the discovery of children with various kinds of talent; and he has served as consultant to several school systems which have developed accelerated learning programs.

As he makes clear in the monograph, Dr. DeHaan is using the term "accelerated learning" to mean an experience of learning which goes beyond the depth and range of learning which the average child accomplishes. He does not mean to restrict accelerated learning to the idea and practice of skipping grades in school or of going through school in less than the usual time, though this is one possible form of accelerated learning.

The concern about the gifted child which has been so prominent in American education since 1950 is treated in this monograph as a solid fact on which better educational programs can be established throughout the country. In a democracy, where all children go to the same type of school and where most children complete secondary school, there is a profound problem of serving the superior children well. The principle that each child should have educational opportunity which is consistent with his potential for learning requires special attention of some kind for the superior child. Furthermore, the number of children who are treated as "gifted" is quite large in a program that is appropriate to a democratic society. It includes at least ten per cent and possibly as much as twenty per cent of the children. Dr. DeHaan shows how the ordinary school system, with ordinary resources of money and personnel, can do a better job of teaching superior children.

Thus, this monograph is written for the entire educational profession of teachers and administrators—not merely for use in a few highly privileged communities.

ROBERT J. HAVIGHURST
University of Chicago

v

Contents

CHAPTER I

Accelerated Learning Programs
and General Education

This monograph is based on two propositions: that human variability exists and should be encouraged, and that every child should be given the opportunity to be educated to the limit of his capacity.

The fact of human variability forces itself upon anyone who deals with learners in the educational enterprise. Even kindergarten children exhibit outstanding differences to an observant teacher. By the time the children reach junior and senior high school, the differences are much more marked.

Differences among children are almost infinite in number. Perception, intelligence, temperament, motivation, biological equipment, rate of maturing, social background—these are only a few of many dimensions on which children vary. In any aspect a teacher considers, he will find that children differ from each other, sometimes markedly.

Let us look a little more practically at some of the differences. In any classroom chosen at random from any school in the country will be found students who are physiologically a year or more older than their classmates. In the same room can be found one or two other pupils who may be biologically as much as a year behind most of their classmates. Some of the children are able to read a book rapidly and deliver an adequate report on what they have read; others laboriously pick their way through the words, and show little comprehension of what they have read. Some children are socially mature, with an almost adult perception of life; others, even in adolescence, are immature and childlike in their outlook. A few have seemingly limitless capacity to learn; others, so to speak, have a low ceiling.

Differences exist not only *among* children, but also *within* them. No child is equally advanced in every skill in all areas of knowledge, or in every kind of interest. John, for instance, may be more physically mature than his contemporaries, his knowledge of current

1

events relatively undeveloped, but his interest in electronics deep and knowledgeable. Jane may dislike arithmetic and perform poorly in it; she may excel in music, but have only a minimum interest in sports.

In this monograph, the fact of human variability is recognized; the position is taken that the variability is a valuable asset to the individual and to the various communities in which he lives. Therefore, individual differences—aside from pathological aberrations—should be encouraged.

There are several reasons for placing so high a premium on individuality. One is philosophical and historical: the right for each individual to be free, to choose for himself—to *be* himself—is a part of our liberal democratic heritage. Another is psychological: the strong urge within each individual to be unique.[1] The third is social: a complex society such as ours needs a variety of talents and many different kinds of persons; it is best served by individualistic persons with highly developed skills and talents.[2]

Educators need to encourage individuality through the programs provided in the schools. American children must be educated along lines that will not only develop their similarities and their common heritage but also bring out their unique combinations of capabilities, aspirations, and personalities. American educators must solve the educational equation without cancelling out the factor of individual difference—in fact, they must maximize that factor.

American educators are meeting the challenge of individual differences in learning through the general provision of differentiated learning programs. Consider the kinds of programs that are provided for just one such difference: speed of learning. All educational programs could be differentiated according to the rate of learning of which the pupil is capable. Let us look at the continuum of such educational programs. At one extreme we find programs for slow-learning children. Such programs have well-defined purposes and are accepted as a necessary and important part of a total school program.

In the center of the continuum is found the general or "common

---

1 Carl R. Rogers, *Client-Centered Therapy* (Boston: Houghton Mifflin Company, 1951).
2 Dael Wolfle, "Diversity of Talent," *The American Psychologist,* XV (August, 1960), 535–45.

learning program" which is suitable for most of the school children in America. The purposes of this program are to educate the children for participation in a democratic society and to give them the necessary vocational skills for making their way in the world. The pace and complexity of learning is geared to that of an hypothetically average student. Other monographs in the Library of Education Series deal more fully with this program.

At the other extreme are the accelerated learning programs designed to provide educational experiences for the rapid learners. Accelerated learning programs are an extension upward of the common learning program.

The provision of accelerated learning programs grows out of the belief in the desirability of encouraging variability and maximum growth among all children. These programs are part of the larger effort to provide differentiated learning programs designed to encourage such individuality and growth. Accelerated learning programs have the same philosophical, psychological, and social bases as programs for slow-learning and average children. They are designed to fit the special capacities and needs of a segment of the school population: the rapid learners. Thus, accelerated learning programs are liberalizing. They free a segment of students to pursue their education without artificial restrictions.

Some people, however, fear both the short- and long-range effects of accelerated learning programs. They fear that the programs will give rise to an intellectual elite, that there will be invidious distinctions made among the children, and that the programs are basically undemocratic. They also fear that a "get tough" academic policy will grow out of the accelerated learning programs that will operate to the detriment of average and slow learners.

Such fears are not completely unwarranted. Abuses and misapplications of the programs need to be corrected if they arise. The fact that such dangers exist, however, is not sufficient reason for failing to do what needs to be done. The fears of the few can serve as a set of cautions that need to be observed. Nevertheless, the overriding consideration is still the philosophical, psychological, and social necessity of establishing and maintaining accelerated learning programs for rapid-learning pupils.

Definition and Characteristics
of Accelerated Learning Programs

The term *accelerated learning programs* is a general one that will be used to designate the provision of learning experiences over and above what the common learning program has to offer. Accelerated learning programs provide more material to be learned at a faster pace, a greater variety of learning experiences, and learnings of more complex and novel nature that require a higher level of generalizing and abstracting ability than is required for the usual educational programs.

Acceleration is a relative or comparative term in several senses. When a teacher uses the term *accelerated learning program*, he is comparing it to some average or standard educational program. There is no hard and fast line where the usual educational program stops and the accelerated program begins.

Accelerated learning programs differ according to the needs of the community which the particular school serves. For example, the accelerated educational program in a professional community where the vast majority of pupils will go on to college would probably differ considerably from that in a large city or rural area.

Compared to the hypothetically average student, bright children learn rapidly. When compared to their own natural pace of learning, however, the rapid learners could hardly be described as accelerated. They are simply learning at the pace which is most suitable for them. Thus, although his learning program may be called "accelerated," it is so only by comparison with that of slower learning students.

In educational literature, the term *enriched educational programs* is often found. Accelerated learning and enriched learning may be seen as two aspects of the same process of providing for human variability, just as two faces of a coin are both part of the same coin. The term *accelerated learning program* emphasizes that learning is to be relatively speeded up. The term *enriched education* emphasizes the necessity of providing a greater variety and novelty of educational experiences. But greater variety cannot be provided unless learning is accelerated and acceleration is usually intrinsically novel and enriching. Enrichment assumes acceleration and acceleration is futile without enrichment. In practice, the two generally go together.

In this monograph, *enrichment* will be subsumed under the term *acceleration.*

A characteristic of accelerated learning programs in America is their multiformity—i.e., they take many different forms. At present there is no standardized acceleration program, nor will there ever be one. Multiformity, as we shall see, grows out of the very nature of the learners who are participating in these programs. Rapid learners exhibit even greater varieties of ability and motivational patterns than do average or slow-learning children and therefore require a greater variety of educational offerings.

Benefits

Accelerated learning programs generally increase the student's motivation to learn. Provision of meaningful, advanced, novel, challenging experiences is one of the important aspects of accelerated learning programs. Such a program is intrinsically motivating to pupils. This assertion has been born out again and again in schools that have established such programs.

Conversely, simple, repetitive, learning experiences tend to depress motivation. This has been observed in school and has also been shown by experiment.[3] One experimenter asked a group of children to make a series of pencil strokes on paper to a given rhythm. Eventually, the children became bored with the task and refused to go on with it, even when the experimenter urged them on. They were then given a new rhythm and told to make more strokes. Again, they eventually tired of it and once more refused to go on. After a few more changes in rhythms, the subjects absolutely refused to make any more strokes. They were satiated.

Although no educator would ever teach such extremely monotonous and low-level skills, the experiment is significant: rapid learners are probably more subject to boredom and to depressed motivation because of repetitive overlearning than are any other children in the classroom.

Accelerated learning programs provide a greater quantity of learning. Rapid exposure to more facts and principles and general-

---

[3] Anitra Karsten, "Psychische Sattigung," *Psychologische Forchung,* 10 (1928), 142–254. Cited in Benjamin Wolman, *Contemporary Theories and Systems in Psychology* (New York: Harper & Row, Publishers, 1960), p. 466.

izations builds up the student's storehouse of knowledge. The accumulation may be imperceptible to the student. In fact, he may not discover that he knows more than others until he enters college, when he has opportunity to compare himself with students from communities which had no accelerated learning programs. Students need to know more today than ever before. As we shall see, the mere accumulation of knowledge is not the only goal of an accelerated learning program, but it is one of the important ones.

Accelerated learning programs enhance the morale of the school. When students become excited about education (as they usually do in accelerated learning programs), when they begin to see the importance of learning, when a school emphasizes achievement and develops a tradition of excellence, a new dimension is added to school life. This dimension might be called respect for the realm of the intellect. The students who participate in accelerated learning programs are often opinion leaders among students. When the opinion leaders evaluate the school program positively and are excited by it, the attitude of other students toward the instructional program also tends to become positive.

Providing accelerated learning programs also challenges teachers. Teaching is often a matter of motivating reluctant learners. In accelerated programs, motivation is much less of a problem: pupils are usually eager to learn. The teacher's task is more a matter of directing learning, providing materials, and making suggestions to youngsters who are eager and capable of learning rapidly. Thus, teaching is transformed from a prodding, plodding, operation to a process of guiding, selecting, and clarifying.

Pupils in the common learning program often benefit from what is being done for and by their more rapid-learning friends. Average pupils often wish to participate in the interesting experiences their faster classmates are enjoying. Teachers can often rather easily adapt the material taught to rapid learners for slow learners and can hold out modified accelerated learning programs as incentives to average students.

The accelerated learning programs are also significant for the community as a whole. In the long run, they pay off by providing the community with better-educated leaders who know more, are better motivated, and have had a stimulating learning experience in school.

Furthermore, if it is true that accelerated learning programs also raise the general morale of a school, then the community benefits by getting a better quality of education for its tax dollar.

Objectives of Accelerated Learning Programs

Objectives of education can be thought of as a pyramid. At the base are the objectives for the relatively small number of slow-learning pupils. These objectives might be termed *subsistence objectives.* Educators expect slow learners to attain simple objectives: developing simple work skills, learning the basic facts of the economy and democratic life, attaining a modicum of human relations skills in order to subsist and to contribute to society at their particular level of training and ability. Most average and rapid learners attain such learnings outside of school—at home, or in the community. The school takes a direct hand in seeing that slow learners attain these learnings in school.

The second level of objectives goes beyond simple subsistence level to the maintenance level. Educators expect average and above-average pupils to attain more complex and advanced learnings, attitudes, and skills. Pupils need to learn how to maintain and operate a democratic government; they need to learn more advanced vocational skills; they need to know how to live morally. Also, many students in the average range of ability will go on to post-high school training and need to obtain preparatory training for it. Rapid learners are expected to attain these objectives but, unlike average pupils, they are expected to go beyond them as well.

The third level of objectives goes beyond maintaining society: it seeks to advance it. This leadership level applies to the relatively small number of pupils in accelerated learning programs. Since students who participate in the accelerated learning programs will provide the major portion of the leadership in years to come, their education should fit them for their role. That is, they must be able to do more than simply maintain democracy: they must be able to advance our civilization.

For this reason, the facts, principles, and generalizations that they are taught should be carefully selected, since even rapid learners cannot be expected to learn everything. They need to learn things that are most pertinent and applicable to the solution of the complex technical, social, and moral problems they face as adults. Students should also be taught the skills of applying their knowledge creatively to the solutions of problems on hand. Finally, the outcomes of an accelerated learning program should be such that students will accept the challenges of leadership that lie before them, neither grasping the privileges of power, nor avoiding the risks of making decisions, nor abdicating the responsibility that will surely be thrust on them.

Below is a list of objectives that have been suggested for accelerated learning programs. It is by no means a complete or systematic list.

1. Knowledge in relevant and important areas of learning, such as science, the operations of democracy, contemporary threats to our way of life, the heritage of Western culture. Knowledge needs to be constantly re-evaluated as to its relevance to the future of Western culture and to the swiftly-moving social scene.

2. Skill in conducting human relations, obtaining factual information, thinking productively, communicating, and organizing.

3. A well-thought out sense of values and a directing philosophy of life which serves as the foundation for exercising responsible leadership, for making choices, and for evaluating courses of action.

There is a good deal of urgency to the matter of establishing accelerated learning programs for bright students. The urgency stems not only from the needs of society but also from the fact that children grow up so swiftly. The period of formal education is relatively short. There is hardly time to teach even rapid learners the many things they need to know in order to realize their full potential. Certainly there is no justification for wasting time or for allowing children to be taught in such a way that their learning capacities are not fully developed.

CHAPTER II

Definition and Description of Candidates

The development of accelerated learning programs is often hampered by difficulties in the terminology used to designate the pupils to be served by such programs. A wide variety of terms has been used. Examples of such terms are: "the gifted," "superior students," "talented children," "rapid learners," "the capable," "academically talented," "students of superior endowment," and "geniuses."

It is not surprising, however, that educators experience difficulty in finding a suitable term with which to designate gifted children. One difficulty lies in the connotation of the term *gifted* and in the value attitudes that educators and laymen hold with respect to it. The term *gifted child* implies a person of greater worth than an average or slow-learning child. It is sometimes found, for example, that a teacher's evaluation of a student will rise if he finds out that the student has a high I.Q., and conversely that his estimation of a student will decline if he finds out that the student has an average or low I.Q.

Try as we may, we cannot escape the fact that gifted children are going to contribute more to society and are therefore of greater potential social value than their less gifted peers.

The tendency to evaluate giftedness highly is opposed by other deeply ingrained values and attitudes. The desire to help the underdog and the belief in the equal worth of every individual are expressions of two such values. Because of this conflict in values, teachers often vacillate between the necessity of coming to grips with the problem of developing suitable terminology and educational programs for gifted children and their desire not to distinguish them in any way from other children. The terms that have been coined to designate the gifted child are another indication of the desire to avoid the value connotations of the term *gifted children*.

There is additional confusion in the minds of some people over the terms *genius* and *gifted children*. When the term *gifted child* is used, some people think immediately of the word *genius*. Gifted

9

children, however, are not necessarily geniuses, although a genius is undoubtedly gifted. Occasionally a teacher's confusion over these terms prevents him from doing anything for gifted students. Because he rightly observes that there are no geniuses in his class, he wrongly concludes that he needs not be concerned with accelerated learning programs, not realizing that there probably are gifted students in the class who need such programs.

The term *genius* is an unfortunate one for discussions of educational matters because it refers to a child most teachers will never encounter. It is well to recognize from the outset that accelerated learning programs are not to be limited to geniuses.

Origin and Evolution of a Definition

Some of our present patterns and problems of defining giftedness stem from the work of Lewis L. Terman in the 1920's.[1] In his monumental study of gifted children, he used as the criterion for selection a Stanford-Binet Intelligence Scale I.Q. of 140. The series of volumes in which Terman's work is reported is entitled *Genetic Study of Genius*. Thus, in the tradition of Terman has risen the notion that children whose I.Q. is 140 or higher might be called geniuses. Children of such ability comprise less than 1 per cent of the population.

The work of Leta S. Hollingworth reinforced the conception that only very superior students should be included in the definition of giftedness. Her work[2] dealt with approximately one child in a million. Thus the early definitions of giftedness were based upon the I.Q. and included only a very small proportion of children. The precedent set by Terman and Hollingworth tends to prevail to this day.

In the late 1920's and early 1930's, Paul Witty expanded the definition of giftedness to include those who are in the approximately upper 10 per cent of the juvenile population in terms of ability and those who possess any talent which showed remarkable promise. Following the same basic line, DeHaan and Havighurst more recently defined the gifted child as one who "is superior in some ability

---

[1] Lewis M. Terman, *et al.*, *Genetic Studies of Genius*, Vols. I-IV (Stanford, Calif.: Stanford University Press, 1925–47).

[2] Leta S. Hollingworth, *Children Above 180 I.Q.* (Tarrytown, N.Y.: World Book Co., 1942).

that can make him an outstanding contributor to the welfare of, and quality of living in society."[3] These authors also distinguish between children in the upper one-tenth of 1 per cent—whom they called the "first order" or extremely gifted children, and the remaining children in the upper 10 per cent—whom they called the "second order" or solidly gifted children.[4] This distinction combined the original ideas of Terman and Hollingworth with Witty's expanded definition.

DeHaan and Havighurst also outlined in great detail the kinds of talents that they included with intellectual ability as measured by I.Q. tests. Creative thinking, scientific ability, social leadership, mechanical skills, and talent in the fine arts were the talents listed.[5] Their concept of first-order and second-order giftedness applied to each of the talent areas as well as to intellectual giftedness.

Thus, the definition was expanded both qualitatively and quantitatively. That is, many talents besides intellectual ability as measured by I.Q. tests were included and a much more generous proportion of children with ability were encompassed under the definition of giftedness.

It is true, however, that the qualitative expansion of the definition to include talents in addition to intellectual ability has never really caught on in American schools. The term *gifted children* is still used primarily to refer to intellectual giftedness. And by "intellectual giftedness," most people mean a high I.Q. as measured by standardized intelligence tests.

The definition of giftedness has recently been expanded further. The Superior and Talented Student Project of the North Central Association includes children in the upper 25 per cent of the student population in its definition of giftedness.[6] In the Demonstration Guidance Program of New York City,[7] the lower limit of giftedness was an I.Q. of 100. Thus the term *gifted child* may mean almost anything from the upper half of the class to the upper tenth of 1 per cent or less, depending on the community and nature of the

[3] Robert F. DeHaan and Robert J. Havighurst, *Educating Gifted Children,* rev. ed. (Chicago: University of Chicago Press, 1961), p. 15.

[4] *Ibid.,* pp. 15–16.

[5] *Ibid.,* pp. 18–19.

[6] "Identification," *NCA Superior and Talented Student Project* (Chicago: North Central Association of Colleges and Secondary Schools, 1958), p. 3.

[7] "Demonstration Guidance Project, Junior High School 43, Manhattan, and George Washington High School," *Third Annual Progress Report* (New York: New York City Board of Education, 1958–59).

program. It may also include children who possess talents other than academic and intellectual ability.

Recently, Gallagher[8] has presented a scheme which may help clarify the problem of definition and terminology. He has suggested that the term *academically talented* be reserved for those whose I.Q. is 116 or higher (using the Stanford-Binet Scale of Intelligence as a reference test). It is important to understand that the 116 minimum was not arbitrarily selected: it corresponds to a statistical measure called a *standard deviation* (S.D.). See the Library of Education volume entitled *Testing Student Achievements and Aptitudes,* by Ahmann for explanation of the standard deviation. Suffice it here to say that the standard deviation of the Stanford-Binet test is approximately 16 points, and that the term *academically talented* is applied to those whose I.Q. is 16 points or more above the average or mean.

In the general school of population, 15–20 per cent of the children have I.Q.'s above 116. In a school serving a community of high socio-economic level, 45–60 per cent of the children may possess I.Q.'s of 116 or above. In a school serving a deprived community, they may comprise only 5–10 per cent of the total. Students in this group are probably able to succeed in college and perhaps successfully engage in graduate work.

The term *gifted* is reserved for students whose I.Q. is 132 or higher. Statistically, this I.Q. measures two standard deviations above the mean. The students found at this level comprise approximately 2–4 per cent of the total school population. In a favored community, the figure might be 6–12 per cent; in a deprived community, perhaps 1 or 2 per cent. Such students can probably do graduate work and earn research and professional degrees.

The term *highly gifted* is reserved for students with an I.Q. of 148 or higher. The I.Q.'s of such youngsters lie three standard deviations above the statistical mean. In the general school population, such youngsters would comprise about one-tenth of 1 per cent of the total. The percentage might be three times higher in a better community and two-thirds lower in a deprived community.

In the scheme proposed by Gallagher, the category of "academically talented" includes the "gifted" and the "highly gifted"; the

8 James J. Gallagher, *Analysis of Research on the Education of Gifted Children* (Springfield, Ill.: Office of the Superintendent of the Public Instruction, 1960), p. 5.

"gifted" category includes the "highly gifted." Such overlap of categories is undesirable because it confuses the educational picture. An educational program for the academically talented students is not likely to be suitable for the gifted or the highly gifted, and a program for the gifted is not likely to meet the needs of the highly gifted.

For the purposes of this monograph, a modification of Gallagher's categories will be used. The term *academically talented* will not include the two higher categories but will be used to designate only the students whose I.Q. is between the first and second standard deviation above the mean, or between 116 and 132. The term *gifted* will not include the "highly gifted" but will be used to indicate students whose I.Q.'s lie between 132 and 148, or between the second and third standard deviations.

This monograph will deal primarily with problems of educating the "gifted" according to the above modified definition. What is said will apply only indirectly and with appropriate modifications to the education of either the academically talented or the highly gifted. The needs of the latter group are so unusual that radical steps must be taken to provide them with adequate education. The needs of the academically talented, on the other hand, can probably be met with only slight modification and acceleration of the general educational programs.

The gifted are the most likely candidates for accelerated learning programs. They have sufficient ability to be generally unchallenged by the common learning program, but they are not so outstanding that they need radically specialized programs.

General acceptance of the above definitions and terminology will do much to clarify the discussion of gifted children and help to define the kinds of accelerated learning programs that such youngsters need. The reader should be cautioned, however, against thinking of these as precise categories. For example, a student with an I.Q. of 128 technically should not be included in the category of the gifted. Yet such a student is more similar to the gifted than he is to the academically talented. In actual practice, as we shall see, the definitions have to be used judiciously, not legalistically.

As has been indicated earlier, however, the concept of giftedness should include more than just intellectual or mental giftedness as measured by an I.Q. test. Herein lies a weakness in Gallagher's definition: it is exclusively an I.Q. definition. There is sufficient evidence on hand to indicate that if only mental ability as measured by an I.Q. test is used to define and select candidates for accelerated learning programs, a sizeable proportion of gifted children will be overlooked. At least four categories of giftedness need to be added to the category of intellectual giftedness to round out the total definition of candidates for accelerated learning programs:

1. Children who show creative thinking ability. This is a type of intelligence that is not measured by the usual I.Q. tests. Creative thinkers are inventors, innovators, originators.

2. Children who have special aptitudes in the fine arts, such as plastic arts, graphic arts, writing, music, dramatics, and dancing.

3. Children with mechanical and craft skills.

4. Children who have high social abilities that are basic to leadership.

A real problem in including the above four categories in an overall definition of giftedness is that there are at present no tests comparable to available intelligence tests for measuring such talents. Although tests for measuring creative ability are being developed, little or nothing is being done to develop valid and efficient tests for identifying abilities in the fine arts, mechanical skills, or social abilities. The tests that are available are crude, difficult to administer, and hard to score.

Consider what the situation would be like, however, if there were a test for measuring artistic aptitude that was as good as the Stanford-Binet Intelligence Scale or the Wechsler Intelligence Scale for Children are for measuring intellectual ability. The prospect of identifying and accelerating artistically gifted children would become much more feasible and attractive to educators. Artistic ability could be defined quantitatively in terms of standard deviations as intellectual ability has been. If satisfactory tests were available for every conceivable human ability, educators could arrive at a truly scientific definition of giftedness. Since there is little social pressure for developing abilities other than intellectual ones, however, there is little hope of developing more than vague criteria for nonintellectual categories of giftedness. They will probably continue to be considered lesser talents.

For the sake of the ideal, however, this monograph will include in the definition of giftedness nonintellectual as well as intellectual giftedness. Whenever nonintellectual talents are the subject of discussion, they will be clearly designated. Unless otherwise stated, the discussion will be understood to refer to intellectual giftedness.

Composite Portrait of a Gifted Student

Consider a composite portrait of a gifted student. The portrait will not fit any specific individual; it is composed of information gleaned from studies of countless gifted children. The portrait may be useful in helping a teacher form a general picture of gifted children, candidates for accelerated learning programs. It may also prepare the teacher attitudinally to accept such children and provide adequate educational programs for them. Let us call the person in our composite portrait Bob.

Bob is deceptively ordinary at first glance. He is not the wizened bookworm some people might imagine him to be. Neither is he a midget wizard performing miracles with his chemistry set. Terman's study[9] destroyed many such misconceptions about gifted children. If a teacher were to look over a group of children walking down the corridor, he would find no physical, social or behavioral abnormality that could distinguish Bob from his peers. Bob would mix in with the crowd: he would be having fun and getting along well with the other boys and girls.

Physically, Bob is somewhat larger, healthier, and better-coordinated than the average child. His interests in sports and physical activities is on the par with other children his age. In short, he is a good physical specimen in the biological sense; and he is socially and emotionally well-adjusted.

Bob is bright mentally. In this respect he is probably most unlike his peers. If he were tested with a standardized intelligence test, he would earn a high I.Q. on it, probably above 132 (by our definition). If Bob were given a test of creative thinking, he would probably score as high on it as he did on the test of intelligence. Being creative as well as highly intelligent, Bob tends to be somewhat less conventional in his behavior than if he had only a high I.Q. and were not creative. He is likely to have a good sense of humor, which he might turn against the teacher on occasion, and perhaps thereby irritate her. Bob is likely to be rather independent of conventional adult

---

[9] Lewis M. Terman, *et al., op. cit.*

values, preferring to do things his own way. He may be considered
by his classmates to have some wild ideas. He is probably able to
achieve well academically. At times he will be persona non grata to
the teachers because his creative splurges and his independence are
not always easy to control by conventional methods. He may resist
routine assignments and insist on doing things differently from the
other students. He thrives best on freedom and on unstructured
classrooms.

The fact that he has a high I.Q., however, does not mean that Bob
will inevitably be creative and do well on a test of creative thinking.[10] In fact, other students who have lower I.Q.'s may surpass him
in creative ability. If Bob is not creative but has a high I.Q., he will
achieve well in school, will fit into the conventional patterns of
school demands, and will be persona grata to teachers. He prefers to
have a well-structured class where the teacher lets him know what
is expected of him. He also likes to be tested regularly so that he
knows where he stands. He probably memorizes well and also does
well on tests.

Because Bob has high verbal ability and is able to master and
comprehend verbal concepts, he is often able to work several grade
levels ahead of other members of his class in areas that require verbal
achievement, such as reading, social studies, and spelling. His reading tastes may be rather superficial, however. He may read books
that are easy rather than difficult. Furthermore, he may be very
articulate verbally, but somewhat glib rather than profound. If this
is the case, Bob may just be reflecting the superficiality and lack of
intellectual excellence in his environment.

His achievement in arithmetic does not seem to be as great as his
achievement in areas requiring verbal ability.

If Bob's mental makeup does not include much creative ability,
his pattern of school achievement may be along conventional lines
of accumulating knowledge, learning the textbook, and getting good
marks on tests. He may have trouble applying what he knows to new
problems. On the other hand, if he does have a large measure of
creative capacity, his accumulation of knowledge may be less but his

---

10 Jacob W. Getzels and Philip W. Jackson, "The Study of Giftedness: A Multidimensional Approach," *The Gifted Student*, "Cooperative Research Monograph,"
No. 2 (Washington, D.C.: U.S. Office of Education, 1960), pp. 1–18.

creative application of that knowledge to the solution of problems may be considerably greater.

Because of Bob's ability to accumulate and manipulate verbal material, he can handle the usual school curriculum with great ease. He is likely to continue to achieve at a high level and to be highly productive even after he leaves school and moves into adult life.

This does not mean that Bob faces no hazards in school achievement, however. If a certain complex combination of factors exists in Bob's family and social background, he may actually turn out to be an underachiever (see Chapter IV).

If Bob achieves well, however, it is because he most likely comes from an upper-middle class family. His father is probably a professional, a businessman, or in some kind of managerial position. In terms of racial and ethnic background, Bob is likely to be white and to come from Jewish or North European background. It is possible, however, that Bob comes from a lower socio-economic level or from a minority group. At the present time it is not clear how much the family background and socio-economic status contributes to Bob's giftedness. Some research shows that the lower socio-economic groups are capable of producing more gifted children than they have in the past. But schools have been less successful in stimulating them than they have in stimulating children from middle socio-economic groups.

In terms of his peer group relationships, Bob is more popular and more socially acceptable than many of his average classmates. He is likely to be frequently chosen as a leader for many kinds of social activities, but he may prefer to shun social leadership and concentrate on scholastic activities and achievement. His high intellectual ability is more of an aid than a hindrance to him in achieving social acceptability.

Emotionally, he is well adjusted and stable. His desire to be independent may sometimes be irritating to adults. If he is noncreative, this desire is likely to be less strong.

Such a portrait represents a person who is, generally speaking, a well-formed, well-integrated, highly productive person.

Many teachers do not easily perceive in their pupils anything that corresponds to this portrait. Instead they see exasperatingly ordinary children who seem to be alternately bored or boisterous, who ask hard-to-answer questions, who seem obstinate, who like to talk about such things as the meaning of life and death, who have superficial study habits, or who shun others. There seem to be more exceptions than adherents to the portrait. "Are these children candidates for accelerated learning programs?" a teacher may ask.

Yes, they probably are. What teachers see is the raw material, not the finished product. Teachers may be misled by glowing descriptions of gifted children found in the Sunday supplement of the newspaper or in the educational journals. What these accounts rarely, if ever, mention is that the youngsters started out bored, noisy, and seemingly ordinary. It is only after years of shaping and polishing that they become the showcase students described in educational journal articles. To bring them to such a high point in achievement and general development is the challenge of teaching in accelerated learning programs.

CHAPTER III

Identification of Candidates

Two general methods are available for identifying candidates for accelerated learning programs: systematic observation by the teacher, and various kinds of objective and semiobjective tests.

A third method is emerging and may have potential value: self-selection by the pupils themselves. The key criterion in self-selection is the motivation of students, assuming that motivation is as important a determinant of achievement as ability is.

How effective are teachers in identifying gifted children? Research conducted to answer the question is inconclusive. What has been rather clearly shown by research is that if teachers are given only vague and unclear criteria of giftedness, if they are not trained to observe children carefully, if they do not have a chance to know their pupils, and if they are not supervised in their observations, there is little agreement between teachers' observations and the results of aptitude tests. It is not clear, however, whether the fault lies with the teachers, with the conditions under which they are asked to rate their pupils, or with the tests that were used as criteria of intelligence. In one study,[1] for instance, teachers were required to identify the "genuises" in their classrooms. No further instructions were given nor were any criteria provided. Under these conditions, only 40 per cent of the pupils whom the teachers identified as geniuses had I.Q.'s of 120 or higher. The childrens' I.Q.'s in this study, however, were measured by group tests which probably give less reliable results than an individually administered test. Thus the tests and the instructions for observation, as well as the teachers' judgments, might have been in error.

It is generally recognized that teachers' observations need to be supplemented by data obtained through objective tests. It also appears necessary to give the teachers training and supervision in what

---

[1] W. Drayton Lewis, "Some Characteristics of Children Designated or Mentally Retarded as Problems, and as Geniuses by Teachers," *Journal of Genetic Psychology,* 30 (March, 1947), 29–51.

they are expected to observe in children. The teacher must be personally well-adjusted and aware of his biases if he is to make accurate ratings. It still remains to be discovered by research what is the best role for teachers to play in the identification process.

When teachers are asked to observe and nominate candidates for accelerated learning programs, they are usually given a guide to follow. The guide usually consists of a list of characteristics that gifted children show. Such lists are rather easy to produce from descriptions of gifted children found in the educational literature.

A list of characteristics shown by children of high intellectual ability might include:[2]

1. Learns rapidly and easily;
2. Uses a lot of common sense and practical knowledge;
3. Reasons things out, thinks clearly, recognizes relationships, comprehends meanings;
4. Retains what he has heard or read without much rote drill;
5. Knows about many things of which other children are unaware;
6. Uses a large number of words easily and accurately;
7. Can read books that are one to two years in advance of the rest of the class;
8. Performs difficult mental tasks;
9. Asks many questions; is interested in a wide range of things;
10. Does some academic work one to two years in advance of the class;
11. Is original; uses good but unusual methods or ideas;
12. Is alert, keenly observant, responds quickly.

Comparable lists have been drawn up to assist teachers identify children with ability in science, leadership, art, creative writing, drama, music, dancing, mechanics, and physical activities.[3]

In addition to observing children's abilities, teachers might also be used to great advantage to observe behaviors which cannot be easily measured with objective tests. Under what conditions does a given student appear to learn most rapidly? What motivational problems does the student have? What things seem to motivate the student most readily? What problems with study habits does the student have? It is in such areas that teacher's observations can probably

2 Jack Kough and Robert F. DeHaan, *Teachers Guidance Handbook* (Chicago: Science Research Associates, 1955), pp. 20–21.
3 *Ibid.*, p. 5.

provide essential information that is very difficult to obtain through objective tests.

An important reason for including teachers' observations as part of the identification process is the effect such a process has on the teachers. The very act of observing children is an essential part of effective teaching. It is surprisingly easy for a teacher to become so preoccupied with behavior problems that she overlooks positive abilities. Teachers become much better acquainted with the strengths of children through careful observation. One teacher said, "Identifying gifted pupils has been hard work, but I know my group better now than any other group I've had." Furthermore, observing and responding to the positive and healthy behavior of children is fully as important for teachers as concentrating on behavior problems. The process of observing children and identifying their talents alerts teachers to the positive abilities of particular children. This side of teaching needs to be emphasized.

The Role of a Teacher in Preidentification of Giftedness

Sometimes the process of identifying candidates for accelerated programs is mistakenly seen as the first step in setting up accelerated learning programs. Giftedness that can be identified by tests or by observation, however, is already fairly well established. The school's problem is already partly solved when children display talent to the point at which identification is possible.

What about potential ability? In bringing talent through this twilight zone of development, teachers can play an extremely important role that precedes the step of identification.

Little is known about the conditions under which various kinds of giftedness originate and come to fruition. Warm, encouraging, personal relationships are probably the very first requisite. Within the child must be found sufficient self-confidence, a certain amount of tension (but not too much), and an ability to trust others and the world in general before he can venture into a new activity which requires a new skill or ability. Teachers can supply the new activities, the trust, the encouragement, and the reinforcement that children need for the first steps toward development of giftedness.

Anyone who has watched a child produce his first bit of artwork is impressed with the delicate balance among the internal and external factors affecting talent development. The child usually identifies strongly with his own work and sees it as an important part of himself. It seems as if something of himself is contained in the scribblings. Undue, premature, and harsh criticism of the child's work will easily upset the balance of factors that made the production possible. In a warm accepting human context in which the child's artistic endeavors are reinforced, the factors will thrive.

Children send up many trial balloons, so to speak, to see if their teachers will accept their efforts for what they are worth. One first-grade teacher for instance, observed a girl playing with something behind her book while sitting with the rest of the children in the reading circle. After class the teacher mentioned that she was interested in what the girl had been doing. The girl said, "Oh, that was Elsa." She then showed the teacher a wooden spoon on which a face and yellow hair had been drawn, and waited for the teacher's reaction. The teacher encouraged the girl to tell of other characters she had created. One by one she laid them on the table for the teacher to see. The teacher recognized the girl's active imagination at work and gave her an opportunity to work on her characters and plays. Other children joined in the activity and creative dramatic talent began to flourish.

If the teacher can look at each pupil afresh every morning without having preconceived notions about what she can expect of him that day, if she can with ease communicate to the class that each pupil has unlimited possibilities, if she can utilize every sign of budding talent, if she is alert to a wide variety of such clues and can allow each talent to follow its own course of development rather than some preordained sequence of forced growth, she can play a most important role in the identification of giftedness.

Before giftedness can be identified and measured, it must be developed. It is in this process that teachers play a most vital role.

Identification Through the Use of Objective Tests

Group intelligence tests are a major instrument for identifying candidates for accelerated learning programs. They are probably more widely used than any other single identifying device—and rightly so: they are the best single device for measuring intellectual giftedness.

General tests of intelligence can best be used as an initial screening device. Since these tests are good predictors of academic success, they might well be called tests of academic ability. Most school systems employ such tests and administer them at regular intervals. Teachers can begin their search for talent by using the scores from these tests as guides. These scores would be found in the cumulative folder.

When children get into junior and senior high school, differential aptitude tests are perhaps more satisfactory than general intelligence tests. Such tests provide a profile of the student's mental abilities rather than a single score. They test more than one intellectual ability and give a somewhat more detailed picture of the strengths and weaknesses of a pupil's mental makeup.

Individual intelligence tests, such as the Stanford-Binet Scales of Intelligence and the Wechsler Intelligence Scale for Children, are well suited to measure the intellectual abilities of children. Such tests must be administered by qualified psychologists and so are relatively expensive to use.

Achievement tests are also widely used to measure achievement in various subject matter areas, such as reading, spelling, arithmetic, languages, and science. These tests have the same general limitations as group intelligence tests: motivational problems may result in spuriously low scores.

Objective test scores and teachers' observations need to be combined in some way. The Superior and Talented Student Project of the North Central Association[4] awards two points to the student if his I.Q. is above 110, or above the seventy-fifth percentile, and one point for each of the following: a score above the seventy-fifth percentile on a standardized achievement test, a grade average of *B* or better, a recommendation by the teacher, and a score above the fiftieth percentile on a standardized reading test. If a student gets four out of a possible six points, he is eligible for the accelerated learning program.

Such an approach for combining scores is desirable. The school system can use cut-off points determined by the nature of the community and the level of ability of the children.

In trying to determine the meaning and significance of I.Q.'s and other scores that are found on a child's cumulative record or that

---

4 "Identification," *NCA Talented Student Project, op. cit.,* p. 14.

are obtained in a testing program, it is advisable for a classroom teacher to consult the school psychologist or someone who has had specific psychological training in the areas of tests and measurements.

The limitations of the objective tests are becoming more clearly understood. It is particularly important to understand that no single score obtained from a group intelligence test can safely be used as the sole standard in selecting candidates for accelerated learning programs. There are several reasons for this. First, group intelligence tests are subject to various degrees of error which can be estimated by the standard error of measurement. Thus, if a student obtains a score of 121 on such a test, his true I.Q. probably lies somewhere within a range on either side of the score. If the standard error of measurement for the test is known, the range can be estimated. If the standard error of measurement is not known, a crude estimate is 10 points on either side of the measured I.Q. In this case, for example, the true I.Q. probably lies somewhere between 111 and 131.

Various group tests differ in terms of their mean and their standard deviations. For this reason, the same score on different tests may have quite different meanings. Furthermore, a different score on different forms of the same test may not necessarily indicate a change in the pupil's I.Q., but rather a change in the form of the test. For example, the highest score obtainable on the California Test of Mental Maturity for twelve-year-olds is 157. On the test for fourteen-year-olds, the highest score is 136. Thus, a pupil might score a maximum on each test and yet "regress" almost 20 points on the second test.[5]

Another shortcoming of group intelligence tests is their failure to identify creative thinking or "divergent" thinking (see Chapter VII). Recent research[6] has indicated, for example, that a student may score rather high on a usual intelligence test and yet be quite uncreative. Another student might score a considerably lower I.Q. and yet be very creative. It is to be hoped, however, that tests designed to correct this deficiency will soon be forthcoming.

Objective tests of intelligence and achievement also tend to be biased against children who come from culturally deprived homes

[5] Gallagher, *op. cit.*, p. 10.
[6] Getzels, *op. cit.*, pp. 1–18.

and social backgrounds. The reason for this bias is that the tests are heavily loaded with verbal items, and the verbal experiences of children from culturally deprived neighborhoods are usually less rich than those of children from professional homes.

Tentative Nature
of Identifying Procedures

The foregoing might easily be misconstrued to mean that the task of identifying candidates for accelerated learning programs is quite impossible. This is not the case. But there is no absolute way of measuring the potential capabilities of those students who can best benefit from accelerated learning programs. The yardsticks available are flexible and inaccurate: they can estimate, but not measure.

The estimates of ability obtained by tests can be refined through the supervised observations of trained teachers. Such teachers can indicate which children they consider to have been underestimated by group test scores. If further confirmation of the estimate is needed, it is probably best obtained through tests—the Stanford-Binet or Wechsler Intelligence Scale for Children—administered by the school psychologist. The whole process might be described as one of successive approximations.

Not every school, however, has a school psychologist available to administer individual tests. Therefore it is sometimes necessary for the teacher to proceed as best she can, even though there may be some question about the accuracy of the estimate of a child's ability. Thus recommendations for an accelerated learning program must be tentative until the identification is confirmed or contradicted by further evidence of the child's learning ability as displayed in the accelerated learning program itself.

The Identification of
Nonintellectual Talents

Although high intelligence probably underlies excellence and high productivity in all fields, it is not possible to identify all kinds of talents through intelligence tests. Identification of a future artist, writer, or leader requires supplementary tests as well.

Additional areas in which talent can be discovered are art, creative writing, dramatics, music, dancing, and mechanics.[7] Since ability in these areas cannot be discovered through paper-and-pencil tests, it is necessary to use what has been called a "work sample." A work sample consists of a drawing, composition, or a performance of some sort which can be judged and compared in terms of others of its kind.

For instance, what can a teacher do to discover children with artistic talent? The first step that the teacher should take is to work with the art consultant who can tell him what indications of talent to look for in children's drawings. Teachers are sometimes tempted to evaluate realism most highly. Art consultants, however, would recommend that teachers look for creative expression, for freedom of movement in the lines that are drawn, for expressive and pleasing use of colors, and for interesting and balanced use of space. With some practice and with some samples on hand (so that the art consultant can illustrate his points), a teacher can learn how to rate children's drawings for creative expressiveness.

The next task is that of devising interesting assignments that will elicit from children their most creative artistic expressions. Such topics as "Fun in the Park," "My Best Story," and "Dinner at Our House" are likely to stimulate children to display their artistic talents.

Each child's drawings should be kept in a separate folder. After giving four or five assignments, over a period of several weeks, the teacher can review the drawings with the art consultant and select those which seem to express the most creative ability.

The teacher might invite the art consultant to watch the children at work. The children who draw well consistently and often could be tentatively considered as having artistic ability.

The identification of creative writing ability follows a similar pattern. The teacher might consult with the language art supervisor or with other teachers to decide upon the criteria for creative writing ability. Teachers should look for such things as originality of ideas, depth of understanding and emotion, choice words, and maintenance of a point of view.

It is important for teachers to recognize the need for temporarily relaxing standards of grammar in order to stimulate original, crea-

[7] See Robert C. Wilson, *The Gifted Child in Portland* (Portland, Ore.: Portland Public Schools, 1959).

tive writing. Attention to grammar can be reserved for later. In the early stages, it is important to encourage the free flow of ideas so that the children are not hindered in their expression by the mechanics of writing. None of the early criteria for creative writing include grammatical rules. These come later.

In selecting writing assignments, teachers should begin with simple problems and work into more complex ones. The first screening exercises might be developing expressive sentences from very simple sentences. For example, a teacher might write on the blackboard, "He threw the ball." She could then ask the children to make that sentence more interesting and picturesque. She might carry the assignment one step further and ask them to write as many picturesque and colorful sentences as they can, using the ideas in the original simple sentence. The sentences that the children write can then be judged according to the criteria of creative writing.

The second assignment might be that of developing a paragraph from a sentence. The sentence might be, "We were sitting around the campfire." The teacher can undoubtedly think up other sentences that would stimulate the children to write a descriptive paragraph.

A third exercise might consist of supplying descriptive phrases and asking the children to write a short story. The phrases might be *cozy fireside, visible castle, brilliant sunshine, creaking hinge, purple shadows,* and so forth. The children are then instructed to take any three phrases and write a story based on them.

A fourth writing exercise might consist of having the class write a poem in the form of the Japanese *haiku.*[8] The *haiku* is a short poem of three lines and seventeen syllables. The first line contains five syllables; the second line, seven; the last, five.

An example of the *haiku* is:

> All the rains of June:
> And then one evening, softly,
> Through the pines, the moon!
> *Oshima Ryota*

Since these assignments are not standardized, a teacher may use any device or assignment she likes. She may also collect samples of

---

[8] Alfred L. Creager, "You can be a Poet Japanese Style," *Woman's Day* (April, 1961), 21.

spontaneous writing that the children compose in leisure moments.

It is important to collect several examples of the poetry and writing of each child. After five or six assignments have been made, the teacher can look over the results and consult with other teachers or with the language supervisor to select the children who show greatest promise.

Dramatic talent can be identified if the teacher provides opportunities for the class to perform pantomimes, improvise, read from script, and use hand puppets. Some of the criteria for rating such dramatic performances are the command the child has of the situation, the hold that he has on his audience, and the extent of his involvement in the performance.

Most schools have ways of encouraging and screening musical talent. School bands, orchestras, ensembles, and private lessons go a long way toward identifying children with musical talent.

Rhythmic ability can be discovered by the physical education teachers, who are also very adept at discovering children who are well-coordinated and strong.

Mechanical ability can best be discovered by encouraging projects that involve construction of some kind. Boys particularly are intrigued by such assignments. If the school has a shop, the shop teacher can help identify youngsters with such ability.

It is interesting to note that mechanical ability is an important correlative of scientific ability. Much of the work of a scientist consists of constructing and manipulating instruments and mechanical devices. A student who has mechanical aptitude is likely to be a better scientist than one who does not—all other things being equal.

Tests for identifying social leadership are called sociometric tests. Sociometric tests rely upon the children's observation and judgment of each other. Children can be asked to rate each other on such characteristics as being able to lead, having ideas for games and other activities, and being able to influence others. Since leadership is an important talent, it is desirable to identify it.

Below is a systematic program for identifying various talents[9] in children, showing when such talents can best be identified.

Schools vary greatly in the amount of formality that accompanies their identification processes. In some schools the identification

---

[9] Adapted from Wilson, *op. cit.,* p. 18.

TABLE 3–1

SCHEDULE FOR TALENT TESTING IN GIFTED CHILD PROJECT

TALENTS	GRADES											
	1	2	3	4	5	6	7	8	9	10	11	12
Art				X		X						
Music				X	X							
Creative writing					X	X	X	X				
Creative Dramatics					X	X						
Creative dance	X		X*									
Social leadership			X		X		X		X*			
Mechanical ability (boys)							X					
Tests of Academic Ability			X		X		X		X			
Achievement Tests				X		X		X		X		
Interest Tests							X					

*Tests are optional.

process is highly systematized and formalized. In one city, for example, a systemwide committee was appointed to review the records of children who were referred by teachers as candidates for accelerated learning programs. The committee helped the teachers to determine the extent to which children can profit from accelerated learning programs and also place the children in special programs if such were available. At the other extreme, and probably far more frequent, are the school systems in which each teacher makes her own independent judgment about the learning capabilities and proper program for each child.

The Role of Personality Factors

It is becoming increasingly apparent that high productivity and achievement depend not only upon intelligence but also upon non-talent factors, which might be called *personality factors*. Most important of these are a strong disposition toward intellectual activities and an interest in aesthetic activities and interests, a tendency to be flexible and non-authoritarian, willingness to take risks in the world of ideas, a greater independence, and a higher degree of confidence and general maturity in interaction with the external world. These are also the characteristics of successful college students.[10]

These factors are noticeable to some extent in elementary school.

---

[10] Jonathan R. Warren and Paul A. Heist, "Personality Attributes of Gifted College Students," *Science* CXXXII (August, 1960), 330–36.

There are no tests that satisfactorily measure all of these abilities in youngsters, however. Much reliance must be placed upon teachers' observations for discovering such nontalent characteristics.

The general importance of recognizing such nontalent factors associated with giftedness is this: teachers can help youngsters who lack motivation and who need help in nontalent areas provided teachers realize the importance of such areas. For example, a fourth-grade boy of high ability was uninterested in schoolwork and intellectual activity. The teacher, who was very friendly but demanding, took special interest in him because he combined high ability with lack of interest in intellectual pursuits. She determined to make mental exercise interesting for him. She went out of her way to discover what his interests were. She talked with him and described what the world would hold for him if he would get to work in school. She helped him develop better study habits; she picked out good books for him in line with his interests and encouraged him to go do the same. These efforts of the teacher grew out of her assessment of the deficiencies in the boy's temperamental makeup, and probably would not have occurred had the teacher not been sensitive to this important factor.

Example of Identifying Candidates for Accelerated Learning[11]

Assume a teacher wants to identify the gifted children in her classroom. What can she do to discover children who are candidates for accelerated learning programs?

Her first step is to examine each pupil's cumulative record. Her school has a systematic program of testing that began in the early elementary grades. Since the cumulative records are kept up-to-date, she has little trouble finding the test scores that she needs for the preliminary screening of her pupils. The records also contain a smattering of anecdoes describing their behavior in earlier grades. These too, help her evaluate their abilities.

Then she consults with the school psychologist and director of guidance for help with the interpretation of some of the scores. If she wants to consider first the top 2 per cent of the children in her group,

---

11 Adapted from Robert F. DeHaan, "Identification of the Gifted," *Education*, Vol. 80 (November, 1959), 135–38.

the psychologist may suggest a "cut-off point," assuring her, however, that there is nothing sacred about it. There is no fixed point on any scale of intelligence or achievement where "averageness" leaves off and "giftedness" begins.

After she has given and scored a group intelligence test and a group achievement test and tabulated results from previous tests, she has in hand data which indicate which children probably have academic talent. If she finds discrepancies in some of the scores, she may ask the school psychologist to administer individual intelligence tests.

Then she supplements the standardized tests with her own observations, realizing that this is a rather tricky method in some respects. She probably would find it easy to discover ability in children who reflected her values and who were doing well in school. She must be careful not to overlook children who do not behave according to her pattern of values and beliefs.

She trains herself to observe all children as objectively as possible, consulting the literature to discover the most important signs of talent. The school psychologist may help her draw up a list of characteristics of giftedness.

One other condition must be present, however, if she is to succeed in discovering the gifts of the children in her room. She must manage her classroom in such a way that a wide variety of challenging opportunities are presented to the children to draw out their talent. If, for instance, she wants to discover talent in creative writing, she would need to provide opportunities and encouragement for her pupils to write with abandon and freedom. If her classroom is run rigidly, with straight rows of desks and straightforward recitation on page-by-page assignments, there is little likelihood that very many different talents would find their way to the surface. The more she seeks to introduce learning experiences that call forth a variety of responses and activities, the more opportunity she will have to observe and identify a number of different kinds of gifts. Only in this way can she break away from the narrow definition of talent in terms of academic achievement alone.

Incidentally, she may find that the principal and even the school custodian can encourage or discourage her from establishing the conditions in her classroom that were needed for the discovery of many different kinds of talents. If her principal frowns on a buzzing classroom, she may not feel like doing much scouting for different talents. And if the custodian tells her that he will not clean her room if the chairs are disarranged one more time, she will probably feel like dropping the whole idea.

This brings us to the consideration of use to which the data from the standardized tests, observations, and on-the-spot tests should be put. It is obviously a waste of the teacher's time to search intensively and extensively for talent if neither she nor anyone else is going to use the results and follow through to provide appropriate learning experiences for children with a variety of talents. The cumulative file is far too often a graveyard for such efforts.

Besides being used to discover unknown or little-suspected talent, the data can be used also to help the pupils understand more about themselves, to help parents and teachers understand the pupils, and to help plan appropriate educational experiences for the children. A child with academic ability, for instance, should be given opportunities to develop his special ability just as a person with musical talent should be given opportunities to study music. Such special educational programs are not always easy to manage and should be undertaken with a great deal of care. The discovery of children with various gifts, however, often serves as a stimulus to broaden the organized curriculum, thereby making it more challenging to more children—even those with average abilities.

Identifying gifted children is a continuous process. A new talent may suddenly begin to bloom in an otherwise average child. The excitement of discovering and nurturing talents in children is one of the most outstanding joys of teaching.

CHAPTER IV

The Curriculum

What advances have been made in the curriculum so as more adequately to educate the gifted child? A survey of the curriculum reveals an uneven development that is in many respects the result of the overriding needs of the times. The curricular areas that were most severely criticized and were most sensitive to pressure in the late 1950's were mathematics, science, and foreign languages. It was in these fields that the greatest amount of research was done and the most profound changes were proposed. There was less pressure for improvement in social science and language arts and consequently less research and less change took place in these areas.

In the fields of mathematics, science, and foreign languages, the speedup of learning can most readily be accomplished. In social science and language arts, however, one would expect horizontal or broad enrichment. Thus, the learning of children whose abilities lie in the sciences, mathematics, or foreign languages can be accelerated, whereas there is a tendency to enrich the learning experiences of children whose abilities lie in social science and language arts.

Accelerated learning programs in mathematics. There is a general feeling that the traditional methods of teaching mathematics need to be revamped. Professional mathematicians paid a good deal of attention to teaching methods in an attempt to discover better ways to teach the subject.[1] The approach adopted by the Commission on Mathematics of the College Entrance Examination Board is a fairly conservative one. The group recommended that the sequence of courses in the secondary level remain approximately as it is, with some upper-level courses added in high school. The greatest amount of pruning would come in geometry. In algebra, more attention would be given to deductive reasoning and to some of the modern theories in mathematics—particularly in the "theory of sets," an important tool for modern mathematics.

---

[1] The studies are summarized in *Studies in Mathematics Education* (Chicago: Scott, Foresman & Company, 1960), pp. 4–7, 59.

Another group, called the School Math Study Group Program, originated at Yale University and was headed by E. G. Begle. It recommended essentially the traditional method of teaching mathematics although much richer content was suggested. This approach and the C.E.E.B. approach described above conserve the basic mathematics as taught at present but bring the curriculum up-to-date with modern mathematics theory.

The Illinois Program, headed by Max Beberman from the University of Illinois, takes a more radical approach. The inductive method of discovery—and the process rather than the content—is emphasized. The program is not as concrete or as closely tied to vocational aims as the more traditional programs have been.

There is some disagreement among professional mathematicians concerning the value of the "traditional" versus the "discovery" method of teaching math. At present, however, such arguments have very little affect on what is going on in the classroom in most American schools, but they may have more profound effects later.

Some of the experiments now underway in the field of mathematics show that it is possible to teach geometry to second-graders, or algebra to fifth-graders. These studies force one to reconsider the notion that there is one and only one way to teach mathematics, or for that matter, any subject. Such a realization, if widely applied, would be of tremendous benefit to children in general and to gifted ones in particular. Nothing is more detrimental to the establishment of accelerated learning program than the idea that there is only one method whereby children can be taught a given subject or skill.

The motivation of students toward mathematics is undergoing a considerable change. At one time mathematics was rather unpopular. In the two decades from 1934–53 there was a decrease in the number of students taking geometry. Now mathematics is becoming more popular. Research by Terman,[2] Cutts, and Moseley[3] indicate that mathematics is often placed quite high on the list of important academic subjects in the judgment of gifted students, although they may dislike it and have to work harder at it in comparison to other subjects.

[2] Lewis M. Terman, *et al., The Promise of Youth: Follow-up Studies of a Thousand Gifted Children* (Stanford, Calif.: Stanford University Press, 1937), pp. 63–133.

[3] Norma E. Cutts and Nicholas Moseley, "Bright Children and the Curriculum," *Educational Administration and Supervision*, 39, No. 3 (March, 1953), 168–73.

It would appear that the best program for a youngster talented and highly motivated in mathematics would be to permit him to move ahead in the field as far as the facilities and personnel of the school allow. He should be limited only by the level at which the teachers can adequately teach mathematics. Four years of mathematics for the academically talented pupil is recommended by Conant.[4] Typical suggestions favor two years devoted to algebra and plane geometry, a third year to intermediate algebra and trigonometry, and the fourth year to college algebra and analytical geometry.

Accelerated learning programs in science. In general, the major change taking place in the teaching of science is that it is being introduced earlier in the curriculum. It is being made a part of the total education of the child, in recognition of the fact that even young children are interested in the world around them and that an understanding of this world is important to their personal and social development. Conant[5] recommends three years of science in the high school. The Bronx High School of Science[6] has one of the best science programs for able students. Seniors pursue special interests in science or mathematics after having spent the first three years in an integrated program emphasizing general education and preparation for post-high school training. Biology and basic courses in physics, chemistry, industrial arts, and mechanical drawing are liberally provided with laboratory work and supplemented by electives and field work.

Below are nine guidelines for the teaching of science to academically talented students:[7]

1. Course content should be developed along lines of contemporary scientific thinking and theorizing. If in the seventh or eighth grade, for instance, the universe or solar system is discussed, academically talented students can consider modern theories of the origin and evolution of the universe, galaxies, and the solar system.

---

[4] James B. Conant, *The American High School Today* (New York: McGraw-Hill Book Co., Inc., 1959).

[5] *Ibid.*

[6] Robert J. Havighurst, Eugene Stivers, and Robert F. DeHaan, *A Survey of Education of Gifted Children* (Chicago: University of Chicago Press, 1955), pp. 14–76.

[7] *Science for the Academically Talented Student in the Secondary School* (Washington, D.C.: National Education Association Project on the Academically Talented Student, and National Association of Science Teachers, 1959), pp. 14–25.

2. Content area should be developed in depth. The emphasis should be upon higher quality of teaching rather than upon greater diversity of subject matter.

3. Continuity of the program should be assured for the talented pupils. Needless repetition should be avoided. In the study of electricity, for example, electrostatics and magnetism might be covered in the elementary school, the electric current in the junior high school, and electromagnetic radiation in high school.

4. Opportunities should be provided for working with scientific materials, equipment, and apparatus.

5. Attempts should be made to reveal and integrate the relationships between the various branches of science.

6. There should be an increasing application of mathematics to the precise formulation of scientific relationships.

7. Stress should be placed upon generalization, development of concepts, broad generalizations, and great issues rather than upon the accumulation of relatively isolated facts.

8. Science resources in the community should be utilized in the teaching of science. Out-of-school programs are a good way to enrich the science program when there are laboratory facilities available in the community.

9. The relationship of science to other cultural areas—such as politics, economics, standard of living—should be emphasized.

Foreign language in the accelerated learning program. Modern foreign languages are offered for varying lengths of time in a student's program. The ten-year program receives the highest recommendation since it permits a student to grow up with the language, and gives him a stronger grasp of it, and exposes him to another culture or civilization for a longer period.[8] If the ten-year program is not feasible, the six-year program is favored over the four-year one.

Young gifted children enjoy the study of foreign languages and generally progress rapidly in it. The study of a foreign language makes special grouping easier because it can be treated as a special interest group. French, Spanish, and German are the languages most usually taught, French being the most popular and German the least of the three.

One of the outstanding features of teaching of modern foreign languages is the functional approach that is given to it in the early

---

[8] Wilmarth H. Starr, Mary P. Thompson, and Donald D. Walsh, *Modern Foreign Languages for the Academically Talented* (Washington, D.C.: National Education Association, Project on the Academically Talented Student, 1960), p. 62.

grades. Foreign language is taught much in the same way that children learn their native tongue, first through listening and talking, and then through reading and writing.

English and language arts in accelerated learning programs. A gradual realization is growing among educators that children learn to read in many diverse ways, just as they can learn mathematics in many diverse ways. There is no single stereotyped way by which all children learn to read. There is also greater recognition of the need for the functional approach for the teaching of language and expression. Thus, in Hunter College Elementary School, oral and written English, written communication, dramatization, speaking, and practice in writing minutes of a meeting are all considered a part of communication and little distinction is drawn among them.

In reading, children are encouraged to broaden their experience and extend themselves into the body of literature. Talented children generally love to read and it takes little to encourage them to read. It does seem to be necessary, however, to help them develop tastes for good reading.

Nevertheless, it is safe to say that the English curriculum generally is undergoing little transformation in the direction of meeting the needs of gifted children. Perhaps the reason is that this subject does not lend itself well to dramatic breakthroughs and speedups, as do some of the areas in which chronological acceleration is possible.

Enrichment in English is accomplished primarily by relating it to other subjects through supplementary activities, correlation with other subjects through extracurricular activities, and use of community resources. There is growing emphasis upon imaginative expression and creative writing for gifted children.

Social studies in accelerated learning programs. There appears to be a general recognition of the need to revise some of the content in the social sciences. Non-Western cultures are being studied in social sciences in addition to the traditional concentration on European civilization. Thus, greater emphasis is placed upon the Asian, African, and Latin American countries. Other new studies—such as psychology, sociology, anthropology, and economics—are being added to some high school curriculums.

Very little has been done, however, to improve the methods of teaching social science. It is probably here that the greatest amount of innovation and experimentation is needed to replace or at least supplement the traditional lecture and recitation method.

One such innovation is suggested by Coleman.[9] The method he suggests is the inductive discovery method. He suggests the possibility of adapting a device called "political gaming" to the study of economics and political problems. In this method, students are organized as groups for the purpose of simulating how nations react to each other in political and economic problem situations. Similar approaches have been suggested earlier by group-dynamics research: the use of role-playing as a device for understanding human relations. These methods have not caught on generally, however— perhaps because they appear to be too artificial or are too difficult for the average classroom teacher to manage.

As one reads of the advances being made in the curriculum, he may be impressed with the tendency of these changes to emphasize the area covered by the first objective for accelerated learning programs. That is, the curriculum changes have been aimed primarily at making the areas of learning more relevant to the swiftly moving social scene and at re-evaluating them in terms of their relevance and importance to the future of Western culture. Thus, in mathematics, for example, there has been a streamlining of content to bring it up-to-date with the rapidly changing requirements of science and technology. Changes in social studies placing greater emphasis on non-Western cultures reflect our greater interest in worldwide commitments and responsibilities.

A Problem-Solving Approach to Curriculum Planning

Visualize, if you will, a meeting of all the educators who are or will be in charge of the education of Bob, the gifted child who was presented in Chapter II. Seated in the group are his teachers from kindergarten through high school; including the principals of the elementary school, the junior high school, and the senior high school; the supervisors; the guidance personnel; the superintendent of schools; and a couple of members of the Board of Education. This group of people will have an influence on Bob's life greater than any except that exerted by his parents.

---

9 James S. Coleman, "Academic Achievement and the Structure of Competition," *Harvard Educational Review*, XXIX (Fall, 1959), 384–51.

Let us present this problem to the group: How do you plan to provide accelerated learning programs for Bob? What recommendations do you have for his curriculum?

This is a difficult question for a group of educators to answer. It is one thing to read reports of unusual accelerated learning programs that are in effect in other schools and to study the procedures and promising practices for educating gifted children; it is quite another thing to apply these principles in the education of real flesh-and-blood children in one's own school system.

Let us not look for unanimity of opinion about Bob's education. There are those on the faculty who will probably advocate a year or two of acceleration as the best solution to Bob's educational problem. Others are shocked at this suggestion and consider classroom enrichment as the only sensible solution. Still others would like to put Bob and other students who have comparable learning capacities into special groups. Others wish to try out new educational procedures, such as "learning by discovery." Still others wish to stay with the traditional curriculum, but make it more difficult. The lack of unanimity reflects some of the controversies that surround the education of the gifted children at the present time.

We turn first to the primary-level teachers, those who teach in kindergarten through the fourth grade. In order to make the question more concrete, let us ask what they would do if they found that Bob was already reading either when he came in to kindergarten or shortly after his arrival. What if he goes beyond the Dick and Jane books in the first grade and begins reading adult material by the third grade? What will be the approach to Bob's reading education?

The most likely answer would be a conditional answer. In short, the answer depends on what reading means to Bob. In other words, *why* does he read? The answer to this question is not as simple as one may imagine. It is usually assumed that a child reads out of healthy curiosity and as an expression of his ability and drive. Other motivations may be mixed in, however. It may be that reading is a way of competing with other children in the class and expressing his superiority. Or it may be that reading is a means whereby he separates himself from other children and places himself above them because he feels inadequate to them in other respects. It is also possible that reading is a way of pleasing his parents and alleviating the pressure they are placing on him at home.

If his reading is a healthy indication of curiosity and ability, the best approach the teachers could recommend is to plan a systematic accelerated reading program for him. In other words, the primary teachers can get together and find books that will further Bob's interest in reading and expand his fund of knowledge. He might be given choices, for example, among books dealing in biography, nonfiction, science and geography, fiction, and poetry. The criteria would be balance and diversity. It would be important for the teachers to cooperate on the planning of such a reading program.

If the teachers become convinced that reading is an unhealthy tendency in terms of Bob's relationship with his parents or with other children, the best approach they could follow would be to consult a psychologist or guidance person to determine what the underlying psychological or social problem is and to try then to resolve the basic problem. This does not mean that Bob would be refused any opportunities to read. Rather, it would mean that he would be given encouragement to read but a search would also be made for the underlying causes of the unhealthy pressures which lead him to reading.

Let us look at Bob in terms of his arithmetic ability. Suppose that in kindergarten he learned the basic processes of adding and subtracting. Suppose that by the first grade he spontaneously began to learn simple multiplying and dividing, perhaps with some encouragement from home. What should the teacher's attitude be? Should she make Bob learn the arithmetic processes as taught by the textbook?

Here the teachers would recognize that there is more than one way to learn arithmetic just as there is more than one way to learn to read. If the child has attained a good mastery of the fundamentals in his own way, the teachers would be satisfied.

It is obvious from the answers of the teachers that they would need to cooperate in any attempt to provide for Bob in the primary grades. Teachers have to work back and forth among grade levels. They have to erase grade lines for Bob. In other words, the third-grade teacher has no set prerogative in her own grade. If the second-grade teacher needs some third-grade materials and experiences in order to maintain Bob's motivation, the third-grade teacher must be willing to allow this to take place without feeling that her grade level is being invaded.

Let us now turn to the intermediate-grade teachers and their supervisors and ask what they might do to move Bob's education forward along the lines begun by the primary teachers. We recall that Bob has developed advanced reading and arithmetic skills, that he is rather widely read for a child of his age, and that he has maintained his curiosity in the primary grades because he has not been subjected to a routine learning process that discouraged the asking of questions nor encouraged blind compliance with adult-oriented and adult-originated rules.

A quick suggestion from the intermediate-grade teachers is that Bob might find a foreign language very stimulating at this age. If we assume that the particular school system represented by the teachers on the committee has a foreign language program in the elementary school, Bob would be released from his class when the group meets in his school. He would not be the only one released since there would probably be other children in the class who also were interested in foreign languages and bright enough to work at them in their early years.

In the intermediate grades, Bob might also be encouraged to explore and probe into different areas of learning. The fourth-grade teacher may offer to help Bob undertake a major project in each of five curricular areas during the course of the year. Biological science might be of particular interest to him, or the teacher might encourage him to do an extended study of the cities that were being studied in social studies. In mathematics he might be encouraged to read about math as a cultural subject. If a specialist in math could be found, Bob might be referred to him for some advanced work. In language arts, he might be encouraged to write creatively and be given as much help as the teacher could provide for him. (She, of course, would also be encouraging other children to write creatively.) In the arts his work would be assessed from time to time to discover what, if any, abilities seem to shine forth. In the fourth grade, it would also be wise to make special efforts to have him develop his study habits.

In the fifth and sixth grades, he would be encouraged to single out those projects that he had undertaken in the fourth grade that have proved most satisfying to him and pursue them further. At this time he would also be allowed to work with children from different grade levels who are interested in the kind of work he is doing.

Thus he would have a chance to organize and to work with them.

The fifth-grade teacher, a man, might take it on himself to talk with Bob from time to time about the meaning of education and what Bob hopes to get out of it. He would encourage him to think along lines of directing his education and learning how to work independently without having to rely upon teachers or other children for his stimulation.

The teachers, in answering the question, face a basic quandry. There are so many possibilities for stimulating Bob that the problem becomes that of selecting the most appropriate ones. Any school system contains people who have specialties, hobbies, or applications of one kind or another. For example, some schools may have heard about a new teaching technique called "inquiry training" and have dispatched somebody to a summer workshop to study it. This teacher returns with a special skill that can be taught to gifted children. Such a person can then be used as a resource for pupils like Bob. Yet no one school system has all of these facilities and resources and the ones that it does possess are likely to be unsystematically distributed in various schools within the system. It requires, therefore, careful planning and organizing to make effective use of sometimes limited and scattered resources and facilities.

The intermediate-grade teachers should be encouraged to check their objectives to see how well and systematically Bob's body of knowledge is growing. What skills is he developing and which does he still lack? Is he beginning to develop a basic confidence in himself and a direction to his life? It is good for teachers to discuss these matters and to look at Bob in the light of the criteria and objectives that have been set up for his education.

In the secondary program, Bob could be encouraged to probe further into new areas of learning, particularly as these areas are set up in the framework of the academic program. He will be encouraged to follow through in his foreign language program, recognizing that he is on the threshold of being able to read the literature and attain a good deal of comprehension of the culture behind the language that he is studying.

Bob will be counseled to take the full academic load, including four years of science, three years of math, four years of English, and the foreign language program.

He will begin an accelerated mathematics program that will cut out some of the outmoded parts of math (particularly in geometry), and in his twelfth grade he will participate with several other bright students in the calculus course.

He can be excused from some of the basic English courses since he knows the structure of the language very well and he will be encouraged to do independent reading, and perhaps to make a research report on some special phase of English.

In connection with the science program, he should be encouraged to make contacts outside of school, particularly with men from the community who work in commercial and research laboratories. If his interests do not follow along the lines of science, but along the field of political science and social science, the school personnel can attempt to find work for him at the local newspaper as a copyreader; or they will help him find a local politician from whom he may learn something about politics in an informal way.

It is possible that some of his work in his last two years of high school will be done in the junior college or in a nearby college.

If the school has a travel-learning program, perhaps Bob can be encouraged to participate in that. He will be given opportunities to partake of the special honors courses although a good deal of attention will be paid to his curriculum to see that he does not become overloaded with work.

Furthermore, the high school faculty will encourage one of its members who has a particularly natural and close relationship with Bob to contact him from time to time to discuss his long-range plans and even get into questions about the meaning of education and the meaning of life. It is recognized that Bob does a good deal of thinking about such questions and welcomes the opportunity to discuss them with sympathetic and understanding adults. He will be encouraged to apply to good colleges, and the faculty will do all in their power to obtain scholarships for him.

Bob can be encouraged to partake in selected extracurricular activities although he probably should not be pushed particularly hard in this area. Much will depend upon the temperament of Bob. If he leans toward social leadership, extracurricular activities will probably have more appeal to him than if he is a studious or creative person.

The faculty should do everything possible to become more than just textbook-teachers to Bob. They must reach out to him and give him opportunities to discuss things that are of vital importance to him.

By making such long-range plans for Bob and thinking through ways of accelerating his learning program, educators can more adequately meet Bob's needs than by piecemeal, spotty planning that considers only one year at a time.

CHAPTER V

Implementation of Programs

Educators generally agree that gifted children should be given an educational program that is commensurate with their rate and level of learning. The major methods available to educators to implement such accelerated learning programs are (1) Acceleration; (2) Grouping; (3) Enrichment; and (4) Community programs.

These methods are related. As was already discussed, enrichment and acceleration are two different sides of the same coin. Acceleration can also be seen as one method of grouping; grouping, in turn, can be seen as a method for making enrichment possible. Furthermore, combinations have been made among the methods that have produced a variety of programs. For instance, community programs can employ acceleration, grouping, and enrichment.

Definitions

The term *acceleration* as used here should be distinguished from accelerated learning programs as defined in Chapter I. It refers to the practice of moving a fast-learning pupil into the curriculum at a more rapid rate. An alternative procedure is to hold the child constant in a given classroom and to move the curriculum to him at a faster rate. The latter method, however, is more like classroom enrichment and is generally referred to as such. Of the three administrative methods of providing for bright students, acceleration receives the most unequivocal support from research studies. Research, however, has not shown a clear superiority of classroom enrichment over special grouping, or vice versa.

Grouping refers to the administrative arrangement of organizing students into instructional units for purposes of accelerating and enriching the learning experiences of the gifted students. Grouping by chronological age is an accepted administrative practice in all schools. Grouping by interest also meets little resistance. Grouping on the basis of intellectual ability or other talent, however, meets much greater resistance.[1]

Classroom enrichment refers to the arrangement whereby the classroom teacher differentiates the curriculum and teaching methods in accordance with the individual differences among his pupils so that they have maximum opportunity to develop their abilities. This method is probably the most common method of providing for the gifted. In practice, it usually involves extending the classroom program for three or four of the better students out of a group of twenty-five to thirty-five.

Community programs are those that take place outside the school program and which supplement it.

Pros and Cons of Enrichment, Acceleration, Grouping

Many of the pros and cons of classroom enrichment, acceleration, and grouping have been discussed in the educational literature.[2] Some of the arguments supporting classroom enrichment are as follows: Classroom enrichment is essential no matter what other accommodations are made. Democratic values are fostered best in the heterogeneous classroom. Leadership training can be carried on more effectively in the average classroom. Since maturation is uneven, the total development of the child can be served better through the varied experiences in the classroom. Gifted children have a much richer experiential background and may be able to provide their own connotations, associations, and perceptions to the usual classroom situation; in a sense, therefore, they can provide their own stimulation. From the financial standpoint, classroom enrichment is the least expensive way to provide acceleration of learning experiences.

Arguments against classroom enrichment in favor of acceleration and grouping run along the following lines: Their presence in the same classroom does not insure that social interaction will occur

---

[1] Robert F. DeHaan and Robert J. Havighurst, *Educating Gifted Children,* rev. and enlarged ed. (Chicago: University of Chicago Press, 1961), pp. 91–106.

[2] Adapted from Harry Passow, "Enrichment of Education for the Gifted," *Education for the Gifted* (Chicago: National Society for the Study of Education, 1958), pp. 201–214. See also Robert F. DeHaan and Robert J. Havighurst, *op. cit.,* pp. 91–113.

among children or that democratic values will be learned. Furthermore, there are many opportunities both inside and out of school for children to develop social contacts and learn the democratic way of living together. Although it is understandable that a teacher likes to have bright youngsters in the class for his own stimulation and for the stimulation of slower children, this is not the responsibility of gifted children. Underachievement is more likely to occur in regular classes because gifted children may develop a sense of superiority or they may fail to evaluate themselves correctly since they have no adequate standard of comparison. Teachers quite naturally spend more time with children who are behavior problems and slow learners, since such children demand more of the teacher while gifted children apparently get along all right without the teacher's help.

Arguments advanced favoring the practice of acceleration follow these major lines: Novelty of learning experiences is needed to motivate the learner. Since bright children learn more rapidly, they need novel experiences at a more rapid pace than other children do. Accelerated learning is not really accelerated for the bright student, but only when it is compared to the pace of average or slow-learning children. By saving a year or two in the total twelve years, a person has a longer productive span, can get married earlier and be self-supporting earlier. Research has shown acceleration to be desirable wherever it has been tested.[3]

Arguments contrary to acceleration indicate that the nature of education is such that time should be spent assimilating it; although certain skills may be accelerated, the process of maturation—on which so much learning depends—cannot. Acceleration removes gifted children from their peers and may constitute hazards to mental and social health. As has been already indicated, however, the arguments against acceleration have been largely refuted by research.

Arguments favoring special grouping are similar to arguments used to oppose classroom enrichment and to support acceleration. On the other hand, arguments against special grouping are similar in many respects to those raised against acceleration and in favor of enrichment in the heterogeneous classroom.

---

[3] Sidney L. Pressey, *Education Acceleration: Appraisals and Basic Problems* (Columbus, Ohio: Ohio State University, 1949).

Beyond Pros and Cons

The time has come to move beyond the pro and con method of discussing acceleration, grouping, and enrichment. These methods have been treated in the past as if they constituted issues upon which battle lines were to be drawn. Advances will more likely be made, however, if they are considered to be problems to be solved rather than issues on which to take sides. All three methods are workable and acceptable under certain conditions. Apparently each method has certain strengths and weaknesses. What is necessary now is to consider the conditions under which enrichment, acceleration, or grouping will be operated most successfully.

Let us consider a few conditions that apply to all three administrative arrangements:

1. Any of the three methods will be successful if there is a determination on the part of the faculty and administration to make it work. So much depends upon the enthusiasm and the desire of the teachers to see a method succeed. By the same token, even the best method can be killed by lack of enthusiasm for it.

2. The faculty must take an experimental, objective approach to the methods that are being tried. Procedures must be constantly appraised in the spirit of experimentation, not of dogmatic partisanship.

3. Paramount consideration needs to be given to the needs of students. When the students' needs are considered carefully, both in terms of short-range and long-range consequences, the faculty is in position to provide the most adequate learning programs for them.

Arguments pro and con should be carried on in the light of individual students. If, for example, a student has demonstrated excellent democratic attitudes toward other students, the argument that he must be left in the regular classroom in order to learn democracy is pointless.

4. Adequate public relations programs must accompany any effort to provide accelerated learning programs in any forms.

Certain specific conditions must also obtain if each of the methods is to be successful. If classroom enrichment is to succeed, the class must be small enough to be handled in terms of the particular competencies of a given teacher. There is no absolutely desirable class size. Some teachers can handle a large class more adequately than others can. The class size has to conform to the teacher's abilities to use an individualized approach when occasion calls for it.

Teachers must take the time to analyze the particular pattern of abilities of their pupils. They must have thought through educational objectives for the bright students, and must have a repertoire of educational devices that are designed to help the students attain these objectives. For given units of work, the teachers need to plan what they will do to extend the learning experiences for the brighter students who can accomplish the units faster than the other students in the class can. To be successful, enrichment should be practiced by all teachers at all levels. It is particularly important, however, in the early grade levels. Furthermore, necessary facilities and materials must be made available along with time for the teacher to plan her program.

There are special criteria for successful acceleration. Before a child is accelerated chronologically, all aspects of his development must be considered. If his total development is adequate, the child can be advanced without detriment. Terman's opinion that children whose I.Q. is over 135 can safely be advanced one to two years in the total twelve-year program is probably still a good rule to follow.[4] Again, research supports this recommendation.

Acceleration can be accomplished in many ways—by allowing a child to enter school at an early age, by combining three years of work into two years, or by permitting the child to go to summer school.

Acceleration seems to be most appropriate in skill subjects, such as reading, arithmetic, and foreign languages, since there is a sequence or progression to these studies. It appears to be less appropriate for subjects that require maturity of judgment, such as social studies, literature, and perhaps language arts.

Special criteria for grouping are as follows: There must be enough students to make up a teachable unit. A special teacher must be available for the students. The enrichment must consist of qualitatively advanced rather than simple more-of-the-same learning experiences.

---

[4] Lewis M. Terman and Melita Oden, *The Gifted Child Grows Up* (Stanford, Calif.: Stanford University Press, 1947), p. 275.

Principles of Enrichment
in Accelerated Learning Programs

In an earlier section of this monograph, enrichment was described as being a counterpart of acceleration. Acceleration cannot be effectively carried out without enrichment and enrichment involves acceleration of learning.

There are countless descriptions of enrichment practices in the educational literature. Most of the descriptions, however, fail to elucidate the underlying principles of which they are but examples. Thus, it is hard to generate further enrichment from the examples that are given or to apply them to another school.

Furthermore, it is important that enrichment be connected with the regular curriculum, the common learning program. Enrichment practices that are not an integral part of the regular curriculum leave much to be desired. They are disconnected, and they lose their effectiveness as a result.

Below are four principles of enrichment that can apply to a wide variety of content as well as to many different grade levels:

1. Change of conditions involving the placement of familiar learnings into different contexts;
2. Reclassification of material into categories other than the usual ones;
3. Discovery of new facts and relationships by experimentation and research;
4. Historical developmental trends in everyday objects.

Changing the conditions under which material is brought into the learning situation is one of the most effective ways of bringing enrichment to the faster learning children. All kinds of conditions can be changed—for example: time, place, and social relations. Three basic kinds of changes of time conditions would be projection into the future, retrospection into the past, and transfer to other contemporary situations.

Suppose that a classroom of children is learning how the earth surface is gradually changing. An enrichment experience for fast learners might consist of the construction of a map of the United States to show how it may look a thousand or a hundred thousand years from now as the earth continues to change at its present rate. Or if children are studying the layout of the school neighborhood on a picture map, they might project what the neighborhood would look like in twenty-five or fifty years. They might, for instance, ask where more homes will be concentrated, where hospitals will be located, and where roads might be built.

Children can retrospect by asking what a person of their age would have experienced in the days of the pioneers, during the Crusades, or in the days of ancient Rome. The teacher might suggest that they write a diary of their imaginary experiences as a creative writing assignment.

An example of a transfer from one situation to another might be taken from a second-grade group that is learning how to tell time. Time might also be measured by the hour glass, by a burning candle, by counting one's pulse beats, and so forth. The group might also be told how time is kept in various countries of the world today.

Reclassification is an important principle of enrichment. In the simple learning situation brighter youngsters can be asked to reclassify in different ways the content of what is being learned. A kindergarten group that is identifying foods by taste and smell might provide the starting point for brighter youngsters to classify in greater detail. Thus, although all apples are sweet, different varieties of apples have different tastes. Youngsters can be asked to classify these. Or if the children are cutting out pictures of "moving objects," brighter youngsters can be asked to rank the objects from the fastest-moving to the slowest-moving, or from those that require the most power to those that require the least power. In fact, the teacher might simply ask them in what other ways the pictures might be classified.

Material can be reclassified in terms of part-whole relaionships. Thus, while average children in Grade 6 are studying the functions of cells in the higher animals, brighter youngsters might be studying the relationships of cells to tissues, of organs to systems, and systems to organisms. They may be asked in what way the whole affects each part and each part affects the whole.

Discovery is an important enrichment experience for youngsters. Discovery can be brought about by means of experimentation. For example, a group of first-grade children may be taking care of plants. Brighter youngsters may experiment with plants by growing some under warm conditions and others under cold conditions, by fertilizing some and not fertilizing others, by growing some under conditions of light and others under conditions of darkness. Experimentation is an important way to discover knowledge.

Second-grade youngsters might be studying how clothing is made in our country. The gifted children might be asked to search in the library for ways that clothes are made in other countries and how they were made in different historical periods. Modern clothes can be compared with those worn in former days. In fact, comparing and contrasting is one excellent way of discovering new relationships.

The historical development of various everyday objects is an interesting enrichment activity. For example, children can be asked to trace how the buttons on the cuffs originated or what was the original purpose and development of heels on shoes.

These principles can be applied to almost any problem. Extra activity on the part of the teacher to apply these principles is one of the ways of stimulating creativity in children.

Community Programs

Community organizations are in a position to extend accelerated learning programs beyond the walls of the school. One advantage of using community-based accelerated learning programs is their comparative freedom. Unlike school programs, they tend to have few restrictions. They are voluntary programs: no child need attend if he or his parents do not choose to. This stipulation releases the teachers from considerable concern about discipline problems, slow learnings, and unmotivated pupils.

Below are criteria for successful community programs:

1. An institutional base is needed. An institutional base makes a program more permanent. In Quincy, Illinois, for example, the Quincy Youth Development Project started its art program in the YWCA. Its drama program began as an independent organization but soon became attached to the Park Board.

2. Personnel for the program must be teachers skilled in some particular hobby or craft for which the program is established. The ability to teach is as important as having a skill or technical ability. Herein lies a problem. Teachers who may be used in a community science program, for example, are often highly skilled in their technical field. Many of them, however, are not necessarily good teachers. Even if they are good teachers, they occasionally feel very uncomfortable within themselves in the

teaching role. They may perceive themselves as being poor teachers. These difficulties centering around the teaching role make it hard to use them in a concerted long-range program.

Sometimes an individual in a community is interested in working with one child over a period of time in a close relationship. Such a relationship is often a highly satisfying one for both the adult and the child.

3. A meeting place is needed. In many cases, such as in a creative writing program, almost any place in which children can write and talk will do. The only materials they need are paper and pencils. In an art program, however, more complicated materials will be needed. For a program such as the dramatics program, even more complex materials and facilities are needed.

4. Selection procedures need to be established. This is particularly important in the community program. If selection procedures are not used, the program can easily become a recreation program rather than a program for developing talent. A very minimum requirement is that the child be interested in developing a particular talent. If some criteria of ability are applied as well, a program can be assured of having children who will be motivated and able to participate in it.

5. Time limits need to be set. Generally, volunteer teaching personnel will more readily commit themselves and their children to a program that has a specified time limit than one that promises to go on indefinitely.

6. A working agreement with the schools must be established. If teachers are aware that their children are in a community program, they can use the classroom to develop the children's talent still further or at least give them an opportuntiy to display their talents. In some cases, special arrangements have to be made for the child to get out of school early or to use some of the school time to work on the project that was begun in the community program.

7. A financial base needs to be established. Generally speaking, although people are willing to volunteer for the early stages of the project, their motivation for the work lags after a year or so. It is necessary to pay people or somehow reimburse them for their time and effort.

Occasionally it is possible to find a small donor or foundation in the community willing to contribute relatively small amounts of money to buy equipment and to pay the teachers a fee or honorarium.

Example of Planning Administrative Arrangements

Consider again the case of Bob, the gifted pupil. Visualize him in the fourth grade. All his teachers marvelled at how quickly he learned and how imaginative and creative he was. In the one group test that had been given up to that point, Bob's I.Q. was 128. He was referred to the school psychologist for individual testing. On the Stanford-Binet, his I.Q. was 148. Bob began to read when he was in kindergarten and seemed to have a special facility for numbers. Taking Bob as a test case, let us see what kinds of administrative arrangements make sense for his accelerated learning program.

If Bob were physically undersized or socially or emotionally immature, it would probably be best to keep him with his own age group until he attained new stature in these areas. If he were mature, well liked, and moved easily in and out of various groups, special arrangements outside the classroom could be made for him, such as chronological acceleration. If Bob tends to be arrogant, competition with his intellectual equals in a special group might be indicated. If he were uncertain of his own ability and unable to see his strengths, it might also be wise to move him ahead or into a special ability group where he could judge his abilities against those of children more nearly like himself. Group dynamics research has shown that individuals do not accurately evaluate their abilities if they have no standard of comparison available.[5]

If the teacher were depending on Bob to stimulate and teach the slower learners in the class, she might have to find some other stimulation for slow learners. Using Bob as a substitute teacher is justifiable only as long as Bob is profiting educationally from the experience, too.

If Bob appeared to be developing habits of laziness, it should not automatically be assumed that he needs greater intellectual stimulation or an accelerated learning program. First, the causes of his "laziness" need to be ascertained. It is possible, for instance, that Bob's laziness is but an unconscious cloak under which he hides his fear of failure from himself as well as from others. Or he may adopt a lazy and bored attitude out of self-defense against demanding parents. In either case, more stimulation and acceleration might only deepen his unconscious defenses. Counseling, guidance, and encouragement from a teacher who could develop a close relationship with him may help him overcome his emotional problems more successfully than an accelerated learning program would.

Even if Bob is achieving at a high level, it cannot blithely be assumed that he should be accelerated or stimulated further. His high achievement may be another defense mechanism serving to hide

---

[5] Leon Festinger, "A Theory of Social Comparison Processes," *Human Relations,* Vol. 7 (1954), 117–40.

his deficiencies in other areas. That is, he may be using high academic achievement to keep himself from having to do other things that threaten him, such as taking part in physical activities or being friendly.

Every condition does not need to be perfect, however, before an educator dares to do something for Bob. For example, Bob might be subject to some social discomfort if he were to be accelerated into an advanced grade level. Should he therefore be held back? He may be just as socially uncomfortable in his present grade, however, in addition to not having the intellectual stimulation that he needs. By being accelerated, he might at least be able to obtain something on which his mind can work, without being any worse off socially.

If in the judgment of teachers, administrators, and parents, Bob needs time and opportunity to think and integrate his many ideas rather than push on to new ideas, acceleration would also probably be out of order. If it were decided not to accelerate him for this reason, then every effort should be made to provide him with the opportunity and stimulation to integrate himself and the world around him.

Since there are so many combinations and permutations of administrative devices, there is no need for an ingenius teacher or principal to feel hampered in providing accelerated learning programs for bright and talented pupils such as Bob.

If the school system is a large and resourceful one, there may be special schools (as in New York City) or special rooms (as in Cleveland) to which Bob can be referred. The teacher can find out and use the proper administrative channels for having Bob examined by the school psychologist for possible inclusion in such a group.

It is not unusual to find schools that have one or more of a variety of grouping plans within their own walls. This may consist of part-time grouping, as in University City, Missouri, or in the Colfax School in Pittsburgh. Under such a plan, Bob would be placed with his own group for much of his work but would join other children of comparable ability for other phases of his curriculum. The groups may be constituted on the basis of interest—as, for instance, a "science interest" group—or on the basis of ability. Favorite groups are foreign language groups. Whatever the basis of selection, Bob would undoubtedly be a candidate.

Schools that have none of the above resources must rely on some kind of grouping within the classroom if Bob is to benefit at all from the stimulating effects of associating with other bright children. Teachers make frequent use of such groups in project work, special study groups, or committees of various kinds. At the very minimum, Bob should be given such opportunities in his own classroom.

Many communities offer special groups designed for stimulating children outside of school. Creative writing clubs (taught perhaps by a former school teacher), opportunities to work in scientific laboratories in industrial plants, and science seminars are examples of community-centered clubs that are available for a student such as Bob. Teachers should become acquainted with community resources of this kind as an adjunct to the school program.

Acceleration can be accomplished in many different ways. Parents may be permitted to present their underage children for examination prior to entry into kindergarten. Thus a bright child may be accelerated by early entry into school. By going to summer school he may be able to graduate a year early. The latter suggestion is an example of a combination of two devices—acceleration and enrichment.

Some communities have available special schools, such as the Laboratory School of the University of Chicago. Acceleration within an ordinary school, however, can be accomplished without great difficulty by allowing a pupil gradually to work into an advanced grade, until eventually he is completely integrated into the new level. Bob, in the fourth grade, might be allowed to participate in the fifth-grade reading and arithmetic programs for the first part of the year. Later he might also join the fifth grade for his science. By Christmas time he might be able to spend all of his time in the fifth grade, making up work from the fourth grade as he went along.

Other schools have ungraded primary groups in which children can accomplish the first three grades at their own speed. Others have adopted variations of the flexible promotion plan, allowing children to do four years of work in three, and so on. School systems that include a junior college have another resource that can be used for acceleration. Bob can do part of his high school work in junior college. Acceleration can also be accomplished in high school through Advanced Placement Classes, or by allowing the student to take extra courses.

There are no limits to classroom enrichment other than those imposed by the ingenuity of the teacher. The teacher's determination to go all out for Bob in the regular classroom is one of the major determinants of the success of providing adequately for him. Perhaps the simplest enrichment device is reading. The teacher will probably have to help Bob select books or his reading tastes may tend to become superficial. Another simple device is to provide extensions of regular units or projects so that Bob can delve into a topic more deeply, do a critical analysis of it, or generalize it to other situations. Free choices help Bob follow his own lines of interest within the context of the regular program. If the teacher is acquainted with new developments in teaching mathematics for example, he might form a small informal group, including Bob, within his classroom for deeper study.

If she does nothing else, a teacher might contact Bob's parents and inform them of Bob's ability. At times teachers are loathe to do this, however, for fear that they will open the Pandora's box of parental pressure. Generally, this fear is unfounded. Most parents are sensible about their children and want to do the best they can for them. They are also generally realistic about what the school can and cannot do. It makes sense, however, to form a team consisting of the home and school in providing accelerated learning programs for bright pupils. The outcomes are likely to be more satisfactory if both parents and teachers are involved in planning and providing for him.

CHAPTER VI

Programs in Action

Brief Historical Sketch[1]

During the past century, the major problem confronting American educators was the provision of a basic education for all children. The schools were given the task of making the dream of universal education a reality. This effort might be characterized as an attempt to provide education in quantity.

Superimposed upon the effort to provide education in quantity was the attempt to provide education to meet the needs of the more able children. Although countless efforts to provide for the educational needs of gifted children were probably made by many concerned, unacclaimed teachers, the first record of a systematic attempt to provide for gifted children took place in 1868 in St. Louis. The plan developed there served as a model until the turn of the century. The plan, called the "flexible promotions system," was basically that of chronological acceleration. Gifted children could complete their first eight years of school in less than the scheduled amount of time without skipping any major parts of the educational sequence. A number of systems—including those in Elizabeth, New Jersey; Santa Barbara, California; New York City; and Chicago—adopted modifications of the St. Louis program. Possibly the most publicized plan for flexible promotion was the Cambridge Double Tract Plan, developed in 1891. The plan permitted bright students to complete the six years between Grades 3 and 9 in four years under the coaching of special teachers. Twenty years later the plan was revised so that students could complete the first eight grades in six years.

The flexible promotion plan continued to be popular through the first two decades of the twentieth century. Significant experiments of various kinds were underway which—although they were incidental to accelerated educational programs—laid the foundation

[1] For an excellent historical review, see Abraham J. Tannenbaum, "History of Interest in the Gifted," *Education for the Gifted* (Chicago: National Society for the Study of Education, 1958.

for variations in the flexible promotion plan and for the development of new programs in the 1920's and 1930's. One of the new developments was the standardized group intelligence test. Because of the necessity of measuring the intelligence of large numbers of draftees in World War I, the intelligence testing movement received a great boost. It became feasible to test large groups of people at once with standardized paper-and-pencil intelligence tests. Group intelligence tests were soon adapted for school use and made it possible to screen large numbers of children in order to identify mental talent.

The work of Terman at Stanford University and the work of Hollingworth in New York, underway early in the 1930's, gave new insight into the needs of the extremely gifted children. These studies were made possible by the development of the individual intelligence test: the Stanford-Binet Scale of Intelligence.

Meanwhile, the developments in the fields of psychology and sociology were shedding new light upon the learning process, the development of personality, the uniqueness of each individual, and the effect the group has upon individual learning.

With growing concern for individuality, the concept of acceleration through flexible promotion began gradually to be replaced by the idea of special grouping. In the 1920's, the Cleveland Major Work Classes, The Detroit XYZ, and the New York City Special Progress Junior High School Classes, as well as some of the special high schools for the gifted in New York, were originated.

A good deal of skepticism, however, was expressed—particularly by child studies specialists—about the feasibility of composing homogeneous groupings of children using mental ability as a criterion for selection. Even when children were comparable in terms of their rate of learning, they were different in so many other ways that homogeneous grouping began to seem a somewhat meaningless term. It was considered advisable to keep bright children within the regular classroom and to provide for their needs there through enrichment.

During the 1930's, there was a gradual decline in the interest in the education of gifted children although some efforts continued to be made to provide classroom enrichment. Interest in the gifted reached its nadir during World War II. The nation appeared to be too preoccupied with many other problems to consider the needs of the gifted.

At the close of World War II, however, interest in the gifted increased once more. Each year there appeared an increasing number of studies and publications dealing with the problem of educating such children. Significant publications began to stir the educational world in the late 1940's and early 1950's. In 1950 the Educational Policy Commission issued a publication strongly supporting the idea of providing more adequately for gifted children. A year later, the volume entitled *The Gifted Child,* edited by Paul Witty, was published by the American Association for Gifted Children. A rash of studies and publications have been forthcoming. Interest shown by the Office of Education and several large foundations in the problem of educating gifted children also stimulated work in this field during the 1950's.

Several factors account for the increased interest in the education of gifted children. Science became one of the fields of competition with the Soviet Union. The need for scientists skyrocketed. The need for scientists was indelibly etched into the mind of the American public with the launching of the Russian Sputnik. It was not difficult thereafter to get a sympathetic hearing for improving the education—not only for future scientists, but for all bright children.

The economy of America began expanding immediately after the war. Many key positions for engineers, scientists, and managerial leaders were created. The needs of the expanding economy came at a time when there was a shortage of young people in their early twenties. This shortage was brought about in part by the low birthrate in the 1930's. A delay in the advanced education of a number of young men in this age bracket who had participated in World War II kept more potential manpower off the market. Still another force toward improving the climate for accelerated learning programs was provided by thoughtful Americans who became concerned with what appeared to be a growing cult of mediocrity. These forces converged on American educators and public in the 1950's and account for much of the current interest in gifted children.

Efforts to educate the gifted during the first half of the twentieth century have therefore been spotty and sporadic. There are outstanding examples of programs to which we may point with pride.

On the whole, however, the efforts have hardly reached the proportions of a concerted movement.

During the 1950's a new high point was reached in efforts to educate superior children. By the close of the decade, the work had taken hold most effectively in suburban communities where a large number of professional people live. In contrast, however, the impact upon schools in the large cities and in small communities was still negligible.

Survey of Contemporary School Programs for the Gifted

Attempts to educate the gifted have gone through a progression of stages that can be roughly designated as acceleration through flexible promotion, grouping of various kinds, and to classroom enrichment. At present, all three approaches are used in various proportions and in various combinations, depending on the school and community. Advocates can be found for any approach or combination of approaches.

Table 6–1 summarizes a number of the programs to educate the gifted that have been instituted in a wide variety of communities across the nation.

Visualizing Accelerated Learning Programs

Perhaps the best way to understand accelerated learning programs is to visit a number of school systems that are making provisions for their bright students. Such a tour should include large school systems, suburban schools, and small village schools. Schools that rely heavily on community resources should be contrasted with those that are practically self-contained. Schools that serve favored communities should be compared with those that serve deprived neighborhoods. And perhaps, by way of contrast, a visit should be made to a school that is doing little or nothing for its bright students.

Such a tour will be provided in the next few pages. Schools will be "visited" for a glimpse at what they are doing for gifted children. The description and actual cases are drawn from the author's files and from the literature on gifted children. The first school to be visited will be an average school which does not claim to have an

TABLE 6–1

SUMMARY OF PROGRAMS FOR THE GIFTED[2]

Community and Date Initiated	Grade Level	Identification Procedures	Educational Provisions	Personnel Responsible for Program	Special Budget
1. LaMesa, Calif. (1957)	1–8	1. I.Q. of 140+ on S-B* or WISC.** 2. Recommended for testing by teacher; high group test scores.	Cluster plan: Gifted children of each grade level are grouped in one room.	The Guidance Department and the Curriculum Department.	None
2. Los Angeles, Calif. (no date given)	Elementary, Junior college	1. "Gifted," I.Q. of 130+; "highly gifted," I.Q. of 160+. 2. Group intelligence tests in Grades 1, 3, 5, 7, 9, 11. 3. Group achievement tests in Grades 3, 5, 7, 9, 11.	Enrichment, acceleration grouping summer school; emphasis on flexible program.	Classroom teacher, guidance workers in elementary school; teacher, scholarship chairman in high school and junior college.	None mentioned
3. San Diego, Calif. (1951, city-wide)	3–	1. S-B I.Q. of 148+	1. Acceleration when desirable. 2. Teacher consultants at elementary and secondary level. 3. Individual counseling and guidance. 4. Study group meetings for parents. 5. Students released from some required courses; allowed to substitute electives.	Special committee	None mentioned
4. Denver, Colo. (no date given, city-wide)	K–12	1. I.Q. of 115+ in first and third grades; retested. 2. Recently substantiated I.Q. of 125; physical and emotional capacity; consent of parents.	1. Guidance and counseling with parents and students. 2. Elementary; individual instruction. 3. Junior high; ability grouping, acceleration, enrichment. 4. Senior high; advanced placement program; guidance.	None mentioned	None mentioned
5. Miami, Fla. (no date given, city-wide)	1–12	1. Grades, I.Q. standardized test scores; teacher judgment. 2. Results of first I.Q. test (given in Grade 3).	Grouping; honors classes; acceleration; enrichment; special programs in math, science, guidance.	None mentioned	None mentioned
6. Winneka, Illinois (1955, suburb)	New Trier Township High	1. Upper 10% of class. 2. For some work, upper 1–2 %.	Advanced placement program; special programs in math, English, social studies.	Superintendent; dean of the faculty; department heads, commit-	None mentioned

	Grade Level	Identification	Program	Administration	Budget
		3. Standardized test results.		...tee on advanced placement.	
		4. Grades in junior high school; comments from junior high school teachers.			
7. Indianapolis, Indiana (1952, city-wide)	5–8	1. Group I.Q. tests in Grades 1A, 4B, 7A; I.Q. of 125+. 2. S-B for referred children and those having I.Q. of 125+.	Twenty-five "gifted child" classes; basic common curriculum plus enrichment, such as French, typing, teacher conferences.	Special Educ. Div. of Pupil Personnel Dept.	$1,550 in 1958–59 for supplementary supplies
8. University City, Mo. (1951, suburb)	Elementary	1. Teacher observation. 2. Results of intelligence and achievement tests. 3. S-B I.Q. of 140+.	1. Enrichment teachers; met with groups 6–10, pupils, Grades 3–6, separately by grade level, 1–2 forty-five minute periods each week. 2. Part-time enrichment. 3. Primary Unit Program; each child, Grades 1–3, to move through Achievement levels at his own pace.	Superintendent; central office staff; school principals.	None mentioned
9. Lyons Falls, N.Y. (1955, rural school)	11–12	None mentioned	1. Youth seminar; pupils brought from all over country on weekly basis. 2. Discussion groups on broad topics—e.g., communication.	District superintendent.	None mentioned
10. New York (1914, city-wide)	4–6	1. Identified at end of third grade. 2. I.Q. of 130+ on individual and group tests.	1. Intellectually gifted children classes; enrichment of curriculum; special projects; special classes. 2. Foreign languages, typing.	Field assistant; superintendent; principal.	None
11. New York, N.Y. Elementary School (1938, city-wide; mostly middle class)	High School of Music and Art	1. Music: Seashore test; judgment of singing and playing. 2. Art: submission of portfolio; situational test.	1. Music: first three years, theory, instrumental, vocal, choral, orchestra music; senior-year elective. 2. Art: first two years, fundamental; last two years, specialized. 3. Complete high school curriculum.	None mentioned	None mentioned
12. Hunter College Elementary School (New York, 1941; complete range but mostly middle income.)	Pre-school 6	1. I.Q. of 136+. 2. Interview with parents.	1. Basic curriculum of New York City Schools. 2. Enrichment provided—Hunter College Campus and New York City.	None mentioned	None mentioned

* Stanford-Binet Intelligence Scale. ** Wechsler Intelligence Scale for Children.

2 Taken from Jack Kough, *Practical Programs for the Gifted* (Chicago: Science Research Associates, 1960), and from Robert J. Havighurst, Eugene Stivers, and Robert F. DeHaan, *A Survey of the Education of Gifted Children* (Chicago: The University of Chicago Press, 1955).

TABLE 6-1 (*Cont.*)

SUMMARY OF PROGRAMS FOR THE GIFTED[2]

Community and Date Initiated	Grade Level	Identification Procedures	Educational Provisions	Personnel Responsible for Program	Special Budget
13. New York Bronx High School of Science, 1938 (city-wide, mostly middle class)	9–12	1. Entrance examination. 2. Past academic record. 3. Ability and interest in science and math.	1. Usual academic high school curriculum; 20% heavier than most schools. 2. Four years English; 4 years social studies; 3 years of one foreign language; 3–4 years math; 4 years science, including laboratory work.	Principal	
14. Cleveland, Ohio Major Work Classes (1922, city-wide but mostly upper-middle class communities)	1–12	1. Teachers' judgment. 2. Standardized tests. 3. Emotional, social stability; good health. 4. S-B I.Q. of 125+.	1. 26 Major Work Enrichment Classes. 2. Enrichment.	Supervisor	Cost per pupil $378 ($275 for regular class)
15. Portland, Oregon (1952, city-wide)	K–12	1. Upper 10% in intellectual and nonintellectual talent. 2. Teachers' observation; group tests; talent tests.	1. Elementary; classroom enrichment; special interest classes. 2. Secondary: accelerated courses, selective seminars.	Supervisor	Five years of outside financial support from Ford Foundation
16. Pittsburgh, Pa. Colfax Elementary School, 1938 (complete range but mostly upper middle class)	K–6	1. Referrals by teacher, parent, child, using all available criteria. 2. S-B I.Q. of 130+.	1. Workshop; homogeneous grouping for academic subjects. One-half of day devoted to workshop. 2. Homeroom heterogeneous grouping for music, art, physical education, and so on. One-half day in homeroom. 3. Type-writing, German.	Principal	None mentioned
17. University of Chicago Laboratory School (no date given, mostly upper middle class)	K–12	1. Average I.Q. of 130; applicants must give promise of being able to achieve at levels of other students. 2. I.Q. and achievement test results; reports from previous; evaluation of social and emotional adjustment; interview with parents.	1. No special program for gifted students. 2. Program varied for individual students. 3. Eight years of work covered in 7 years; after eleventh grade, student is ready for college.	Principal	

accelerated learning program for rapid learners. Such a school will serve as a baseline against which comparisons can be made.

A visit to Average City School. We enter the school and move directly to the principal's office where we are greeted by the principal. He invites us into his office and after exchanging pleasantries begins to brief us. The first point he stresses is that there are no geniuses in his school. Most of the children are average children; although, to be sure, some children are above average. He believes in classroom enrichment. The teachers in the classroom are responsible for enriching the learning of each of these above-average children. The community, he explains, is a working-class community. The parents want a good solid education for their children but no frills. The real problems are lack of rooms and facilities, bringing the slow learners up to par, and keeping behavior problems of children within manageable bounds. Gifted children can get along all right by themselves, he thinks.

Then he tells us that the children have settled down in their classrooms by now, and he invites us to take a look at what is going on in his building.

Our first stop is the kindergarten. The room is really too small, as most kindergartens go. There are two teachers and 60 youngsters in the room. The youngsters are sitting around at the moment, waiting for things to begin. As we walk around, watching the children, we noticed that one of the boys is trying to put a puzzle together; other boys are trying to put together some parquetry blocks. A couple of bright boys and girls have picked up books. When we ask them what they were reading, they go through the books and read passages aloud.

One of the kindergarten teachers mentions with a good deal of pride that the youngsters in this kindergarten are taught only to read their own names. No other words are taught them. When we ask why she didn't believe in teaching the youngsters how to read, her comment is that the children aren't ready for it yet. "How about some of the bright children?" we ask her. She stands on her judgment that they are not yet ready to read. Later, the principal— who has listened in on this conversation—qualifies her answer by saying that if the youngster does read, he is given the opportunity to do so.

In the first-grade room, we notice that the children are seated in a semicircle around the teacher, with books on their laps. The children and the teacher are busy reading about Dick and Jane. The principal tells us that the teacher is working with the slowest group of children. She always takes them first, he says. She feels that they are at their best and can get most out of her instruction early in the day. The rest of the children, about two-thirds of the class, are scattered around the room. Some are coloring or making things with clay. The rest of the children are rather listlessly engaged in one activity or another.

The second grade provides an electrifying contrast. The children are busy studying simple machines. They have already constructed a number of such simple machines. These youngsters are moving freely about the room and discussing what they know about machines. Models of machines are displayed on a table. On the wall is a chart with a definition of a simple machine. According to this definition, a machine moves things together, moves them apart, or changes their direction. The teacher tells us that the children helped discover and formulate this definition by observing what the machines did.

On the wall is another chart showing six basic machines. We ask one of the little girls to describe these machines for us.

"When you come right down to it," she says, "there are really only two kinds of machines. One is an inclined plane and the other is a lever. All of the other ones—the wheel and the screw and the wedge—are just a variation of these two basic machines." Another youngster chimes in at this point to say that a screw is really just an inclined plane wrapped around a stick.

After leaving the second-grade room, we realize that we had hardly noticed whether the teacher was in the room. We hurry back to thank the teacher for her courtesy only to find that she is deeply engrossed in a conference with a student, and evidently had hardly noticed our coming or going.

The third grade is extremely large and is housed in an all-purpose room. A temporary partition has closed off a stage. The principal cites this as one of the bad examples of overcrowding but assures us that an election would be held in the Spring for a bond issue to pay for the construction of four additional classrooms.

The fourth, fifth, and sixth grades are a blur of sameness. Children are sitting in straight rows. The teachers generally dominate the room, standing in front of the group with books in their hands. In the intermediate grades we see a larger boy or two slouched in his seat, smoldering. When we ask the teachers about these boys, they answer that they are slow learners who have great difficulty with their school work and who have been retained at least one year already.

Lunch time gives us an opportunity to talk with the teachers. We find that they are more inclined to be pleased about the progress made by slow-learning children than by that made by any other children. The teachers show a good deal of frustration about "behavior-problem" children. "What can I do with such a boy?" is a question that they ask again and again.

The teachers tend to be interested in practical questions of the how-to-do-it variety. They are little interested in principles underlying practice or in long-range problems. The principal talks incessantly. He is little interested in hearing the observations of the visitors but more inclined to bombard them with his own problems and with the difficulties that he experiences in running his school.

The second-grade teacher is on the fringe of the group. When we ask the principal about her, he shrugs his shoulders and says that this is her last year at the school. A poor disciplinarian, he calls her. She has attended a summer workshop and will probably be offered a teaching position in a suburb of a nearby metropolis.

In such a school as this, accelerated learning programs can at best be but a sporadic, informal operation carried on by one or two plucky teachers.

A visit to Hillcrest Elementary School. The second school on our tour is a suburban school near a large city. The school serves children from an upper-middle socio-economic level.

The principal leads us into a lounge just off his office. His secretary comes in, carrying individual pots of coffee on a tray. While we drink our coffee, the principal briefs us on the kinds of children that come to this school. He tells us his school serves children from professional and managerial classes. The school has about six hundred pupils and two or three sections for every grade. The principal explains that this school is concerned about the gifted pupils but does not believe in special grouping except for French, music, and science clubs. Classroom enrichment, he believes, is the way to handle the gifted.

The first stop we make is in the first-grade room where the teacher is helping the thirty children write a creative story. She has just told them a story about an empty and sad house that stood on a hill. A family, passing by, looked at the house and saw how sad it was. "The father said to the children—"—at this point the teacher stopped and told the children to write their own creative endings. We scatter among the children and watch them. There are many differences in the endings the children are writing, as could be expected. One boy erases his work again and again in order to make it perfect. Other children write avidly; still others write only a few words. Others look in dictionaries to learn how to spell words. Others run up to the teacher and ask her how to spell words.

We are impressed with the large amount of material and facilities in the room. Shelves are loaded with books. Other shelves have such scientific apparatus as an aquarium, tinker toys, and tools. The walls are covered with papers and on these papers are instructions for various things for the children to do as well as much of the work of the pupils themselves. On the blackboard is a plan of action for the day.

At lunchtime, the teacher shows us the stories. Most of them are along the usual theme of the father suggesting to the children that they move into the house. The house, upon hearing this, becomes happy again. There are some very original variations on this theme. In one, the house is given a personality and feelings: tears run down the sides of the house when it cries; the windows smile when it is made happy.

The more we talk about it, however, the more the teacher could see the difference between a creative story and a rather unoriginal one, even though in the latter more words may have been correctly spelled.

In the second section of the first grade there is a research table at which a number of children are seated. These children are raising questions upon which they want to do research. One of the boys, for example, is studying animals that hibernate in winter. The question he is trying to answer is: "Why do animals stop hibernating and wake up in the spring?" He has looked through all the books at his grade level and has come to the conclusion that he will have to turn to the encyclopedia because he cannot find the answer.

Herein lies a dilemma for a number of bright children. They ask such advanced questions that they are not able, with their present reading skills, to find the answers to them. The books they can read do not deal with such profound questions. Therefore, teachers must help them break down their more complex and profound questions into simpler ones to which they can find answers. The teacher is beginning to point out to these youngsters even at this early age that finding answers to some of these questions could occupy the rest of their lives.

We go on to the second grade where the teacher is holding a group discussion with her youngsters on "Signs of Spring." They are noting the signs of spring they have seen on their way to school, such as insects, animals, birds, plants, and bursting buds. They review what they learned in the autumn about why leaves fall. Now they are discussing why leaves begin to bud. The teacher uses the Socratic method: she directs their thinking by asking questions which they answer if they can. There is very little inductive reasoning, however, and very little use is made of hypothesis at this level.

We hasten on to the third-grade class. The children have just begun a research problem on "How to Attract Birds to the School Grounds." The committees have just met to discuss how to go about solving the problem and have listed a number of procedures which the teacher has written on the chalkboard.

Now we enter the science center room, a fabulous facility for an elementary school. The room contained a variety of equipment and materials for teaching science, such as globes, simple machines, simple musical instruments, and molecular models.

Later we visit a fourth-grade class. There the teacher is conducting a lesson in science on hot lands, dry lands, grasslands, and forests. The children are just beginning work on the cold, dry lands and are listing the kinds of animals that could be found there. Again we note that the plan for the day is written on the board so that the youngsters are aware at all times of what they are supposed to do. If they complete one project early, they can move on to another.

We now go to a fifth-grade room where the teacher is working with a group of youngsters on creative stories. Each youngster has a portfolio of stories. One of the boys reads his best story and then reads one on which he wants help. The youngsters contributed their criticism and suggestions, all of which are to the point. The freedom and the desire to excel displayed by these youngsters is remarkable; yet throughout they seem willing to help each other.

The teacher has solved the problem of the relationship between critical and creative thinking as it applies to writing. She encourages the pupils to be creative in the first stage of their writing. The only directions she gives them are to be free and original in getting their ideas across. In the second stage of writing, the critical stage, they are required to make their writing perfect in form as well as in content.

After watching this group, we hurry on to another fifth-grade group. These children are working on time and space problems. There are twelve large globes in the room, most of which have come from the science center. Two or three youngsters are studying each globe. They are trying to resolve certain problems such as the number of rotations the globe would make in a given amount of time and the distance covered in each rotation. The slowest youngsters make up very simple problems; the bright youngsters make up complex ones.

The sense of excitement is strong at this school. Children are inquiring into one aspect of their environment after another. Teachers are animated, intrigued with the way children learn. Their questions show their sophistication. They have read the latest educational ideas to be found in journals and books. The principal rewards teachers who show originality in teaching. Facilities and materials are available for almost any project. Classroom enrichment is used and there is no question about its effectiveness. The whole school is geared to the process of making learning an interesting and rewarding mental enterprise.

A visit to a Thomas Jefferson High School. Our visit to Thomas Jefferson High School begins in the guidance office, from which the program for superior students is coordinated. The director of guidance quickly points out to us the difference between high school and elementary school. Since a teacher in the high school sees as many as 150 students a day, it is very difficult for her to plan the close personal contact with students that can be found in the elementary school. For this reason, the guidance department coordinates the students' programs.

The director leads us to a bank of files and pulls out a cumulative folder from the section for superior students. He opens the folder, (the student's name is David) and shows us the records that have come from the elementary and junior high school. The student shows a long history of high achievement. Various group tests have found his I.Q. to be between 125 and 148, depending on the test that was used. Aside from a small dip in his average during junior high school, he has consistently obtained good grades. His objective achievement test scores are also consistently one-and-a-half to two years ahead of his grade level.

The student is now a senior and has participated in four years of honors work in English. He has recently also added an honors section in physics. (Two honor sections are all that are permitted to a student in this school.)

We ask the counselor if we may talk to David. Ten minutes later, Dave is in the counselor's office.

We ask Dave whether he is working on a special project in his English class this year. He says he is not. Last year he worked on a project on the influence of existential philosophy on American writers. Although he went into the problem rather deeply, he feels that he should read more broadly this year and so is trying to make as complete a survey of English novelists as he can.

In physics, he explains, he is working with two other students on a project involving taking photographs of reactions in a cloud chamber. His explanations of the technical difficulties involved in the project soon leave us far behind. He explains that although his study is in the field of physics, it also involves advanced work in mathematics since the solution of some of the problems require a knowledge of calculus.

When we ask how many other students are able to do the kind of thing he was doing, David quickly names ten other students (out of a class of approximately two hundred) who are also involved in advanced work. David says he has been informed that the work they have been doing will qualify them for advanced placement in college next year.

A visit to the physics class indicates that it is run on a project basis with relatively few lectures. The classroom is practically empty. Students are clustered at various tables in the laboratory, some with sliderules in hand, others with equipment, some with notebooks.

A tour of the school reveals a well-stocked library which also contains several small seminar rooms and individual study booths. The laboratory facilities are extensive. The guidance director informs us that all science courses are laboratory courses. The language laboratory is a busy place. The director also mentions that about three-fourths of the students go on to college. Many of the parents are college graduates, and a large number of them hold advanced degrees.

A visit to New York City's Manhattanville Junior High School PS–43.   If we had visited Manhattanville Junior High School prior to September, 1956, we would have found that many children left school as soon as possible so as to earn money with which to help support their families. The ratio of pupils planning or actually going on to college was very low. Many of the children came from Brooklyn. Many had no fathers. Others came from motherless homes. Approximately 1500 students came from a deprived neighborhood which is about 40 per cent Puerto Rican, 45 per cent Negro, and 15 per cent mixed.

If we had looked at the test results made by children from this junior high school, we would have found that the median I.Q. was slightly above 80 on group intelligence tests that were heavily loaded with verbal items. One nonverbal test was given: the median I.Q. was 100. The nonverbal test indicated that although the children might be deprived and retarded in some areas, their presumed "native" intelligence was probably close to normal.

In September, 1956, the Board of Education initiated the "Demonstration Guidance Project."[3] The goals of the project were:

1. To identify possible candidates for college who up to this point have not been identified;
2. To stimulate able students who were not thinking of college;
3. To create the aspiration for college education in the minds of students;
4. To educate the community and the parents to accept the idea of a college education as worthwhile;
5. To plan a teacher-training program and get the wholehearted cooperation of the faculty;
6. To guide the pupils and their parents through an extensive and intensive group and individual guidance program;

---

[3] *Demonstration Guidance Project Third Annual Progress Report* (New York: New York City Board of Education, 1959).

7. To provide remedial work in order to bring the students up to and beyond grade level;

8. To raise the cultural level of the pupils in the community.

It was decided that approximately the upper 50 per cent of the student body would be included in the experimental group. The basic principle was to include any student who might possibly have academic potential.

The regular course of study used throughout the city was followed in this school, but greater emphasis was placed upon careers and career-planning. This emphasis was needed to broaden the horizons of the pupils.

The students in the experimental group visited research centers, professional schools, and hospitals near and around New York City. Here they saw for themselves what possibilities were open to them. Such experiences stimulated them to think of college and created aspirations for a college education.

In our visit to the school now, we notice that many students are taking remedial reading and remedial arithmetic. Many are also taking remedial speech.

A number of students are listening to a recording of an opera. Others are viewing a filmed version of the opera. Later, these same students will attend a performance at the Metropolitan Opera House. Afterwards, they will listen to a recording of the opera once more and then discuss it.

Much of the education in this school is conducted after school hours and on weekends. Part of the education consists of visiting colleges, touring the laboratories, seeing the dormitories, and generally getting the "feel" of a college campus.

Part of the efforts that are going on outside the school to accelerate the learning of the students are interviews with parents. Daytime meetings for parents are held and attendance at them is gradually increasing.

One of the very interesting and significant side effects of the project has been the decrease in delinquency and misbehavior in the school. Apparently the excitement and promise of education has gotten through to the students and made all of them more susceptible to the school program.

A community program. Community-based programs have come and gone. Because they are not tax-supported, their life cycle tends to be short. The Sciences and Arts Camps[4] project is a relatively new venture. It is chosen for description because its organization and program represent a good example of a community based accelerated learning program.

The purposes of the SAAC project are to enable youngsters (from the fourth grade on up) to increase their joy in learning and to cultivate their pursuit of excellence in a camp atmosphere during the summer and in after-school follow-up activities throughout the school year; to expose these gifted individuals to new intellectual and creative experiences year after year through early adulthood; and to assist them—when necessary—in their relationships with their families and their schools through year-round guidance counseling. To achieve these purposes, the children are exposed to an enrichment program supplementing and complementing the school curriculum.

Eventually the project hopes to enable gifted children living in one region of the United States to spend their vacations at SAAC establishments in other regions, and to send gifted American youngsters abroad on an exchange program.

A Greenwich, Connecticut, clergyman and four other Greenwich citizens incorporated SAAC as a nonprofit educational organization in 1958. School superintendents in the seven municipalities in the area notified parents of the project. SAAC secured from the Board of Education in Darien, Connecticut (the geographical center of the participating communities), the facilities of its high school for a summer day-camp operation.

The choice of master teachers, junior counselors, and campers was the responsibility of the SAAC educators' committee. The master teachers presented SAAC with a draft outline of a five-year summer enrichment program in their respective fields. The purpose of this draft was to define and articulate new areas of enrichment education, designed to supplement the traditional school curriculum without duplicating any phase of the SAAC program of previous summers.

The program included all the subjects covered the first summer: science, mathematics, Russian, creative writing, creative dramatics,

---

[4] *Sciences and Arts Camps, an Evaluation of its Pilot Project* (New York: Science and Arts Camps, Inc., 1961). Mimeographed.

literature, world politics, American democracy, art and music appreciation and participation, and individual and group athletics.

The main task of the junior counselors was to provide a relaxed camp spirit. They led songfests, camp fire discussions, square dances, group athletics, indoor games, and field-day activities.

Parents who felt their children might qualify applied to the educators' committee. The applicant's principal and teacher filled out a form and sent it directly to the SAAC committee of educators, which used this information as a basis for accepting or rejecting the applicant.

The fee for the summer camp of 1960 was $180. This included transportation to and from camp, supervision of the year-round follow-up program, and daily refreshments. An additional nineteen dollars was charged for registration, insurance, and materials. The first summer's budget was met only partially by the campers' fees; the deficit was covered by borrowed funds.

Three major criteria were used to select those children whom the committee of educators felt had the potential to benefit from the program: intelligence test scores (both individual and group test scores were used); achievement test scores; and teacher evaluations, which were basically structured in form (but the teacher was also encouraged to write an unstructured personal evaluation). The third criterion enabled children of lesser I.Q.'s but of proven leadership ability or of high academic achievement, to enroll in the SAAC program, while the first criterion encompassed many underachievers.

The assorted intelligence test scores which SAAC received from school authorities gave no good basis for adequate comparison of potential ability. Since the children were drawn from seven different school systems, there was wide variation in the kinds of tests and in teacher evaluations. However, SAAC's retesting of all campers during the summer with a standardized instrument indicated that the campers fell between the ninetieth and one-hundredth percentile of the country's population, with a median around the ninety-fifth percentile. The mean I.Q. was 134.

A total of 216 campers enrolled in the first summer's program. Thirty attended on scholarships. About 5 per cent of the campers could not profit from the camp program because of personal adjustment difficulties requiring long-term intensive counseling. The ratio of boys to girls was about 2:1.

The campers were organized into groups which were named after colleges. Placement was determined by the camper's grade level. The groups were subdivided on the basis of individual interests.

It was found that interest groupings for the sixth-grade students worked well. However, the evaluations of the master counselors indicated that it is far more difficult to identify effectively the true interests of the fourth- and fifth-graders. Furthermore, experience revealed that it is best to have all groups coeducational, since all-boy groups had more difficulty in adjusting to the program.

Each group was exposed to all phases of the program. However, each group had a free period of about eighty minutes each day during which its members were allowed to participate individually in any activity—pursue particular projects in any of the subjects, utilize recreation equipment, play the piano, play chess, take part in team sports, or apply to any master counselor for additional guidance in a given subject area. The leisure activities were supervised by junior counselors.

Freedom was a unique characteristic of the SAAC program. It expressed itself in several ways: the freedom to pursue an individual project within the structured subject-matter area (e.g., science, math, art); the freedom to select from a wide variety of supervised activities (e.g., chess, newspaper, athletics, sketching, Russian folklore) during free time; the privilege of dropping one subject-matter area, upon directors' approval, to intensify study in another (sixth-graders seemed to have the maturity to assume this kind of responsible choice, whereas fourth- and fifth-graders needed more guidance in exercising their freedom); the program's emphasis on the individual camper rather than on the group, enabling each child to develop and progress at his own rate.

Evaluation of Accelerated Learning Programs

A variety of accelerated elementary and high school programs, ranging from plush suburban schools to inner-city schools, have been described in this chapter. These were contrasted with a school that had a very ordinary, uninspired program of education.

An important question needs to be asked now about the effectiveness of accelerated learning programs: What are the outcomes of these enterprises for children who participate in them?

We must unfortunately begin with a disclaimer. Research designed to measure the effectiveness of accelerated learning programs is uncommonly difficult to conduct successfully. The main reason for the difficulty is the multitude of variables that are involved in the educational process: ability level, motivation, past educational history, family background, socio-economic level, teaching methods, content, and the relationship between teacher and student. These variables need to be controlled if research is to tell us anything definitive. Establishment and maintenance of control groups, however, is particularly difficult in the usual public school situation. It is almost impossible not to "contaminate" the control group with the methods used with the experimental group. Finding adequate and sensitive instruments to measure change is a crucial problem that still remains unsolved. These factors combine to frustrate all but the most skillful and persistent researchers.

In view of these difficulties, it is not surprising that little good evaluative research has been conducted. Eckstrom[5] after reviewing a number of studies says: ". . . inability to control the type of teaching and failure to provide differentiation of teaching according to ability levels are important weaknesses in most of these studies. Another factor which has affected these studies has been poor experimental design. . . ." An analysis of research in teaching science[6] describes the research as "fragmentary . . . of narrow local interest and limited application."

In spite of the difficulties of conducting research on the subject and the weakness of the results obtained, it is possible to draw some conclusions about the effectiveness of accelerated learning programs.

With respect to achievement, it appears that special homogeneous grouping is of questionable value. Ekstrom[7] reports that about half the studies she surveyed favored homogeneous grouping and about half of them did not. Perhaps better research would yield more positive results, but we cannot be sure at this time.

[5] Ruth B. Ekstrom, *Experimental Studies of Homogeneous Grouping: A Review of the Literature* (Princeton, N.J.: Educational Testing Service, 1959), pp. i–ii.

[6] Ellsworth S. Obourn and Charles L. Koelsche, *Analysis of Research in the Teaching of Science, July, 1956–July, 1957* (Washington, D.C.: U.S. Office of Education, 1959), p. 40.

[7] Ekstrom, *op. cit.*, p. i.

When special programs are evaluated in terms of motivation and creative expression rather than academic achievement, it appears that positive results are perceptible. Barbe,[8] for instance, in evaluating the Cleveland Major Work Program, found that opportunity to express individuality was one of the features of the programs most highly praised by pupils who had gone through them. Sumption[9] found that participants in the major work classes engaged in a wider range of self-expressive activities than did those who had not participated in the program. Goldberg[10] found that an accepting, flexible teacher who was effective in group work was able—within the span of one school year—to increase to some extent the motivation of underachieving gifted students.

Chronological acceleration, as has been hinted at earlier, has been demonstrated to be an effective method of dealing with gifted children. Findings by Worcester,[11] Pressey,[12] Justman,[13] and others indicate positive results from chronological acceleration as it is carried on in many different forms. The Ford Foundation[14] conducted an experimental program in which high school students were admitted to college before they had completed their high school education. Careful evaluation of the program strongly suggests that the advantages of early admission to college greatly outweigh the disadvantages.

One important accelerated learning program that has been evaluated positively by its spreading acceptance and growth among both secondary schools and colleges is the Advanced Placement Program[15]

---

8 Walter Barbe, "Evaluation of Special Classes for Gifted Children," *Exceptional Children,* 22 (November, 1955), 61.

9 Merle R. Sumption, *Three Hundred Gifted Children* (Yonkers-on-Hudson, N.Y.: World Book, 1941).

10 Miriam Goldberg, *et al.,* "A Three-Year Program at DeWitt Clinton High School to Help Bright Underachievers," *High Points,* 41, (1959), 5–35.

11 Dean A. Worcester, *The Education of Children of Above Average Mentality* (Lincoln, Neb.: University of Nebraska Press, 1955).

12 Sidney L. Pressey, "Acceleration: Basic Principles and Recent Research," *Invitational Conference on Testing Problems* (Princeton, N.J.: Educational Testing Service, 1954), pp. 107–12.

13 Joseph Justman, "Academic Achievement of Intellectually Gifted Accelerants and Nonaccelerants in Junior High School," *School Review,* 62 (March, 1954), 143–50.

14 *They Went to College Early* (New York: Fund for the Advancement of Education, 1957).

15 *Advanced Placement Program Syllabus* (New York: College Entrance Examination Board, 1958), pp. 7–16.

of the College Entrance Examination Board. In this program, college-level courses are offered in high school. Examinations in these courses are administered by the Educational Testing Service at established centers near the end of the school year. Students who pass enter college with advanced standing and credit. The positive evaluation of the program is evidenced by the increasing use being made of both the program and the testing service that accompanies it. In 1954, eighteen schools had 532 students in the program. They took 959 examinations and entered 94 colleges. In 1955, the numbers increased as follows: 38 schools, 925 students, 1522 examinations, and 134 colleges. These figures continued to increase in subsequent years.

The very cursory review given above does not do justice to the amount of research carried on in an endeavor to evaluate accelerated learning programs. The interested reader is invited to pursue further the research literature cited above and in the general bibliography.

CHAPTER VII

The Learning Process

As every educator knows, the heart of education is what goes on between teacher and learner. The relationship between teacher and learner is the crucial factor. To be sure, the curriculum, facilities, teaching materials, administrative arrangements, and community values are important in providing the physical and social setting in which education in general and accelerated learning programs in particular can take place. The many provisions and arrangements. however, can only provide the context for but never take the place of the teacher-pupil relationship.

In a book about accelerated learning programs, the factors affecting this relationship need to be thoroughly explored. Because of its fundamental importance, it will be explored in two aspects, both of which are important to the success of accelerated learning programs. First, theories about the learning process itself will be examined for what they have to say that will help teachers better understand what goes on in accelerated learning programs. Second, the interesting and significant problem of stimulating creative thinking will be discussed in relationship to accelerated learning programs.

Theories about the Learning Process[1]

Learnings processes are complex—so complex that it seems as if several completely different and unrelated kinds of learning can be found. Psychologists who have studied the learning process have proposed many theories about how learning takes place.

There are two specific groups of psychological theories about how learning takes place, plus a third which is only indirectly related to the question. Most of the diverse and often contradictory concepts of learning can be encompassed by these three groups of

---

[1] Adapted in part from Ernest R. Hilgard, "Learning Theory in Its Application," *New Teaching Aids for the American Classroom* (Stanford, Calif.: The Institute for Communication Research, 1960), pp. 19–26.

theories. The first is the *stimulus-response* tradition in psychology. S-R theory deals primarily with responses in the learning situation. The second is the Gestalt tradition, also called *cognitive theory*. Cognitive theory deals with the perceptual and thinking processes that take place in learning rather than with the responses that indicate what has been learned. The third comes from studies of personality. The approach to learning drawn from studies of personality deals with such things as emotions, motivations, and the social aspects of learning.

Principles of learning from S-R theory. Let us first look at several principles of learning that can be drawn from S-R theory.

1. In order to be learned, the desired responses should be reinforced or rewarded. The nature of reinforcement has been studied more intensively and extensively by S-R learning theorists than by any other group of psychologists. Some of the earliest experimental work on animals was done in order to discover the nature and conditions of reinforcement. Professor Thorndike's famous cats, for example, were rewarded with food for escaping from their puzzle box. Thorndike believed that the reward stamped in the cats' nervous system the "correct" responses—that is, those responses that were instrumental to the satisfactions of the cat's internal needs.

The importance of reinforcing in the classroom the kinds of behavior that satisfies the pupil's needs and that teachers desire is obvious. It is difficult, however, for teachers to control reinforcement effectively because in order to be effective reinforcement should follow desired behavior by a few seconds or less. Teaching machines and programmed learning are designed to provide immediate reinforcement for desired behavior. The machines are constructed in such a way that a pupil discovers almost immediately whether or not he has given the correct answer. The immediacy of the discovery is reinforcing. There is no delay as there often is when teachers give progress tests or hold classroom discussions. Thus, the pupil's responses can be shaped by the use of immediate reinforcements on the lines along which the teaching machine is programmed.

In accelerated learning programs, too, many occasions arise for the application of reinforcement in the learning situation. If creative thinking is desired, children need to be rewarded when they show evidences of such thinking. This may at first involve the reinforcement of very tentative—almost imperceptible—creative behaviors.

If high achievement is desired, children need to be reinforced immediately when they make even small efforts in the direction of achieving. We shall see how important this principle is in the later discussion of underachievement.

2. Repetition leading to overlearning is indispensible for the learning of high-level skills such as typing or playing the violin. There is no substitute for frequent repetitions. The old adage—"practice makes perfect"—still holds.

If one accepts the proposition that certain kinds of skills and the knowledge of certain facts ought to be learned to the point at which they become automatic, then there is clearly a place for repetition in accelerated learning programs.

Thus a teacher needs to be selective in what he expects to be overlearned in accelerated learning programs. Research, however, has tended to support the idea that more able children need less repetition than average or slow learners do in such areas as reading, spelling, and arithmetic.

3. Teaching should be conducted under a variety of conditions for maximum transfer to take place. Some of the very early studies on learning showed that animals could generalize their response to a number of different stimuli provided the new stimuli did not differ too drastically from the original one. For example, a dog can learn to respond by lifting his paw to the sound of a bell ringing at a given tone. The dog can learn to respond to different tones of the bell or to different intensities in sound. In general, however, the more the tone or intensity differed from the original conditions, the weaker was the dog's response. It should be noted that this kind of generalization does not require understanding.

Educators are more interested in verbally mediated generalization of understanding and transfer of training rather than "stupid" generalizations found in animal studies of generalizations. Examples of a variety of kinds of generalization can be gathered easily from any classroom. Suppose a teacher wants children to respond to the word *C-A-T* by saying *cat*. He wants them to say *cat* whether the word is written on the blackboard, or on a slip of paper, or printed on a page in a book. The teacher needs to provide the variety of situations in which the word *cat* can be used by the children.

With respect to the speed and breadth of generalizing, candidates for accelerated learning programs far outstrip their slow-learning friends. Bright children are able to discover the similarities in stimuli that superficially, at least, appear to be very different from each other. The ability to penetrate into what appears to be a divergency and discover in it a similarity is one of the mental characteristics of bright children. They also excel in the ability to transfer what was learned in one situation to another. The existence of ability to generalize in this sense is one of the reasons why it is important to establish programs of accelerated learning for bright youngsters. They need the opportunity to make such generalizations without being continually restrained by the inability of slower children to do so.

Because so much of learning requires discrimination as well as generalization, it is necessary for the teacher to provide a variety of contexts in which discriminative learning takes place. The process of discrimination is an important one, particularly in the teaching of such things as reading. Besides learning to read the word *cat* under a variety of conditions, children need to discriminate the word *cat* from *hat* and from all other words, even though the words are written on the same kinds of cards with the same kind of ink, or written with the same color chalk on the chalkboard.

4. Learning is an active process. Since the S-R theory of learning emphasizes responses, it follows that this theory would emphasize the important fact that learning occurs most readily when the learner is actively involved in the process. "Learning by doing" is still an acceptable maxim of education.

This principle emphasizes the necessity of organizing accelerated learning programs so that even gifted students become actively involved in the learning process rather than being merely passive recipients of factual information. The principle does not mean, however, that everything that is learned must be learned by direct experience. Much can be learned vicariously. The emphasis is rather on the *process* by which a fact is learned, a generalization made, or a skill attained. Learning occurs when the individual is himself engaged in manipulating thoughts rather than hearing others do so or when he himself operates a new instrument rather than simply observing another person do it. It is the learner's mental activity, not the teacher's, that counts.

5. Incidental learning probably accompanies most other kinds of learning. Incidental learning is learning that takes place without

formal instruction and without discernible motive on the part of the learner.

Incidental learning is important to accelerated learning programs in two ways. Incidental learning of boredom or frustration may occur, for instance, while a teacher is busily "teaching" the lesson that was assigned. Fear, too, may be learned incidentally. A teacher may teach arithmetic in such a way that even bright children become fearful of having wrong answers or anxious about failing. The negative emotional reaction to arithmetic was learned incidentally because it was part of the total teaching situation, although the teacher may not have been mindful of it. Later, the negative feelings that have been learned incidentally may arise to interfere with learning of advanced mathematics, for which the learning of arithmetic supposedly prepared him.

Incidental learning has important positive applications, too. Trial-and-error learning is important because of the incidental learning that probably occurs. While trying out one blind alley after another in the attempt to discover the solution to a problem, the pupil incidentally learns many facts, relationships, and applications that are likely to be of great use to him later. In fact, it was shown that chimpanzees who were allowed to play with sticks were later more likely to get the insight of using the sticks to reach fruit than chimps which had not had such experience.[2] Thus, incidental learning that comes during trial-and-error learning can become the raw material from which new insights into new problems will later arise. Incidental learning can be seen to be very directly related to the teaching of creative thinking.

Sometimes, however, undue value is placed on having learners move directly from the statement of a problem to its solution without taking any side excursions or without entering blind alleys on the way. Trial-and-error learning is thereby discouraged and with it the opportunity to learn things incidentally which would assist later problem-solving. One of the beneficial aspects of enrichment in accelerated learning program is that it probably increases the amount of incidental learning.

6. Control of the stimuli or management of the learning is largely in the hands of the teacher. The S-R theory implies that by control-

---

[2] H. G. Birch, "The Relationship of Previous Experience to Insightful Problem-Solving," *Journal of Comparative Psychology*, Vol. 38 (1945), 367–83.

ling the stimuli and reinforcement, the responses of the learner can be controlled. S-R theory emphasizes the necessity of getting the learner to pay attention to the stimuli to which the teacher wants him to attend. Part of teaching lore is to develop techniques to win and hold the attention of the learner to the stimuli the teacher has selected and to reduce the number of extraneous stimuli that distract the pupil from what the teacher wants him to learn. Through the process of calling attention to the important stimuli and reinforcing the responses that the teacher wants, the teacher can "shape" the behavior of the student along desired lines.

Principles of learning from cognitive theory. Certain principles of teaching can also be drawn from cognitive theory. What does cognitive theory have to say about the learning process?

1. The processes of perception and thinking are so closely related as to be virtually inseparable. When a person perceives his world, his mental apparatus is engaged and his perception is determined largely by characteristics of his mental processes. By the same token, a person's thinking is dependent not only on what he perceives, but is also patterned after perceptual processes.

Suppose a teacher makes the following demonstration to a group of students: He lights a candle and after the flame is burning brightly, he inserts a large nail into the tip of the flame. He asks the students two questions: "What has happened?" and "Why has it happened?"

If a formal division were to be made between these two questions, as is so often done in education, the answer to the first would fall primarily in the category of perception, the answer to the second in the category of thinking. They are better thought of, however, as one continuous process. Thus, the answer to the second question obviously depends on answering the first. Not so obvious, yet of utmost importance, is that the answering of the first question also depends upon answering the second one.

A student, for example, might not perceive that the nail was held in the *tip* of the flame—a crucial perception—if he had not thought that the nail might be somehow related to the smoke arising from the flame. Such thinking directs his perception. He may now ask the teacher to hold the nail in the lower part of the flame so that he can see if smoke rises from the flame as it did when the nail was inserted into the tip of the flame.

Psychologists interested in cognitive learning emphasize this intimate relationship between perception and thinking.

2. As many perceptual aspects of the learning situation as possible need to be made available to the learner. One of the earliest criticisms of Professor Thorndike's famous cat experiments was that the cats did not perceive the connection between the string that they had to pull and the door which then opened. It was argued that the cats could have solved the problem of getting out of the puzzle box much more readily had they been able to perceive and understand the connection between the string and the opening of the door. By the same token, the student in the candle-nail demonstration might not have been able to think accurately if the teacher had not presented all the conditions for him to perceive.

The cognitive theorists state the matter something as follows: Whenever one is looking at an object or a picture, the thing upon which he is focusing is called *the figure*. The context in which the figure is presented is called *the ground*. Teaching must be such that the figure stands out clearly from the ground. If it does not, the learner is unable to inspect the crucial relationships, the what-leads-to-what kinds of relationships in the learning situation.

Generally speaking, bright children are much more able to perceive the crucial relationships in the problem. Thus, while the teacher is attempting to clarify the figure-ground relationships for slower-learning children, the brighter youngsters have usually already perceived these.

3. Novel and complex stimuli are inherently motivating. They lead to curiosity and exploratory behavior. It has been demonstrated, for instance, that if a rat is placed in the starting alley of a T-shaped maze and is allowed to enter one arm of the T, the chances are high that on the second trial the rat will enter the other arm rather than re-entering the first arm. This is called *spontaneous alternation*. The rat was satiated, as it were, with the stimuli in one arm and turned to the other in an effort to provide itself with new stimulation.

It is not necessary to look at laboratory evidence in order to be convinced of the importance of novelty in learning. The value of developing exploratory behavior in pupils—particularly in bright students—cannot be overemphasized. If, however, the complexity is excessive or if the novelty is too great, surprise and disruption occur in the learner and may even lead to fear and rage responses.

One of the teacher's important tasks is to pace the stimuli in such a way that they are increasingly novel and complex. In this way the teacher can assure herself of increasing the motivation of the pupil to learn.[3] One of the problems that rapid learners face is that of having too little novelty in their learning environment. Accelerated learning programs are designed to correct that deficiency.

4. Motivation influences perception. This principle has been tested by experimentation in a number of different ways. It appears, for example, that pupils will actually search out stimuli that are emotionally positive for them. It has also been found that individuals will defend themselves from perceiving stimuli that have negative emotional connotation for them.

For example, individuals who achieve well in school have been found to recognize more easily words that connote attainment and goal-seeking than are pupils who are not highly motivated to achieve. Subjects who were hungry were able to recognize words that were related to their hunger more easily than were subjects who were not hungry. People who were highly motivated to affiliate with others were more sensitive to pictures containing people in them than they were to pictures that did not contain human beings. And in a classic experiment, Bruner and Goodman[4] presented coin-sized discs to children from poor homes and to children from wealthy homes. Children from poor homes tended to overestimate the size of the discs in comparison with children from wealthy homes.

5. Learning that is accompanied by understanding of the learning task is more permanent and can be more widely transferred than is rote learning or learning by formula. For example, when students are given a reason for what they are expected to do and shown how their learning task is related to the broader picture of their education, they learn more readily what is required of them. Furthermore, if the learner can discover relationships for himself, and if he is encouraged to make applications of what he is learning, the transfer of what he learns to new tasks will be increased.

6. If the learner is allowed to set his own goals, his motivation

[3] William N. Dember, *The Psychology of Perception* (New York: Holt, Rinehart & Winston, Inc., 1960), pp. 341–73.

[4] Jerome Bruner and Cecile C. Goodman, "Value and Need as Organizing Factors in Perception," *Journal of Abnormal and Social Psychology*, Vol. 42 (1947), 33–44.

for learning is increased. However, children need practice in setting reasonable goals for themselves. The first efforts to do so may result in goals that are too high to attain or too low to elicit sufficient exertion.

The sixth principle has obvious application to accelerated learning programs. When gifted students have the opportunity to think through and decide their goals for themselves, they are more likely to extend themselves to achieve those goals than when the teacher, parent, or some other person makes the goal-decisions for them.

Principles of learning from studies of personality. Many of the following principles drawn from studies of personality do not appear in formal theories of learning because many psychologists who study learning perform their experiments on animals. Since animals lack personality in the human sense, the importance of personality was not demonstrated by animal experiments. Studies of personality are drawn primarily from the field of clinical psychology rather than from the laboratory.

1. The history of the learner must be considered when education is planned for him. Thus, the developmental history of the gifted students must be taken into account when accelerated learning programs are established for them. This point was already touched on in the discussion of cognitive theory, in which it was pointed out that motivation affects perception. When, for example, in a given student's personal developmental history there are indications of conflict with authority, the student will probably have disturbed relationships with the teacher if the student perceives the teacher as an authority figure. It is also conceivable, however, that a previous history of good relationships with authority may facilitate learning in an authoritarian classroom. There are many other applications of this principle.

2. Closely related to the above discussion of the study of the learner's history is the proposition that the social background of the student must be taken into account. The social background of a student will affect even such things as his score on an intelligence test. Davis and Eells have shown that the usual intelligence tests are heavily loaded with verbal items which may discriminate against children from lower socio-economic levels whose verbal experience is less rich than that of children from middle and upper socio-economic levels. The former are likely to make lower scores on such tests, as was found in the Demonstration Guidance Project in New

York City. In other uses of intelligence, for instance, in mechanical problems or spatial visualization or other nonverbal problems—the ability of children with low verbal ability may be as high or higher than children of high verbal ability.

3. A person's self-concept is an important determinant of learning. Self-concept refers to a person's view of himself and his way of thinking about himself. A person who has a low estimate of himself —that is, one whose self-concept is negative—is less likely to try out new and difficult situations than is a person with a positive self-concept. When the person with a negative self-concept does venture into new situations, he is not likely to try hard enough to succeed in it. Each additional failure reconfirms his low estimate of himself.

Self-concept seems to be developed from two sources: (1) the individual's appraisal of his abilities and achievements irrespective of what others think of him, and (2) the internalized evaluations that others make of him. A backlog of success tends to develop a positive self-concept within an individual—both because of his own positive judgment of himself and because others are also more likely to evaluate him positively.

However, with all the selectivity that occurs in perception, it sometimes happens that a person of quite high capabilities and even with a rather large backlog of success, judged in objective terms, may still judge himself to be inadequate. He may filter out and devalue positive evidence of himself and select only signs which indicate his failure.

Such organization of motives, beliefs, values, and perception are particularly important in working with bright but underachieving students whose concept of themselves is generally very low.

4. Threat and anxiety have differential effects on students. Children vary in the amount of anxiety that they either bring into the learning situation or generate within themselves there.

Estimates of the level of anxiety in a student can be obtained. Sarason[5] has discovered that there is a negative correlation between reported test anxiety and I.Q.—that is, the higher the test anxiety, the lower the I.Q. is likely to be. This relationship holds not only for students who have very low I.Q.'s but also for children in the

---

[5] Seymour B. Sarason, *Anxiety in Elementary School Children* (New York; John Wiley & Sons, Inc., 1960).

upper I.Q. brackets. Even in college where high I.Q. students are most likely to be found, students with releatively low I.Q.'s have higher anxiety than do students with relatively high I.Q.'s.

Sarason also found that children who have little anxiety do significantly better in problem-solving situations than children who are highly anxious. Just the opposite relationship is found when the experimenter offers to help the children in a problem-solving situation by giving them more time and giving them hints. Highly anxious children take advantage of the offered help. Children who have little anxiety tend not to bother to accept such help. The highly anxious child is the one who will be at the greatest disadvantage in situations in which he has to decide for himself how to respond. Even though such children have fairly high intelligence, it is not likely that they will be able to use their potentialities in a creative and productive manner.

It appears that anxiety facilitates some kinds of learning,[6] particularly some very "low-level" learning, such as simple conditioning. Anxiety may also facilitate rote learning. Anxiety evidently focuses the attention of the learner and reduces distraction from irrelevant stimuli. Such focusing facilitates learning how to spell or how to memorize the multiplication table. Although the reduction of stimulation from irrelevant stimuli may be necessary to facilitate the conditioning of an individual, it is not good for problem-solving in which stimulation needs to be increased and a variety of solutions have to be sought.

6. The social context in which learning takes place influences learning. Learning in the classroom is not the simple laboratory learning from which theories of learning have been derived. The classroom is a social situation, and is much more complicated and less easily controlled. The way the teacher handles the learners as a group will have much to do with the kind of learnings that can go on and the kind of incidental learnings that take place.

Issues and Problems Raised by Theories of Learning

Educational issues and problems are not resolved by theories of learning. But some of the issues are more clearly outlined.

---

[6] B. R. Bugelski, *The Psychology of Learning* (New York, Holt, Rinehart & Winston, Inc., 1956), pp. 461–64.

One of the first issues that strike a person who studies contributions of theories of learning is the conflict between the necessity of providing novel stimuli to increase motivation and the necessity of providing repetition and drill to produce overlearning. This conflict is especially acute in accelerated learning programs. In order to develop or increase complex skills, the pupil needs to overlearn. Yet, the monotony of overlearning is a threat to motivation. A teacher may find gifted students the first to rebel against repetitive drill. At this point ingenuity is the order of the day. Somehow, she has to be able to introduce enough novelty into the practice to sustain the motivation needed to continue with the drill.

Another issue arises over the nature of teaching. Who should control the stimuli? Should the teacher be the one who controls them and thus reinforces desired behavior? When students attend to what the teacher demands and respond according to what the teacher reinforces, how does this differ from animal training? Or should the teacher start within the perceptual framework of the students and expand it from there in directions desired by the students? The latter view is a therapeutic view of teaching. It lies within the tradition of personality studies and cognitive learning whereas the first approach lies within the S-R tradition.

When are principles derived from S-R learning most applicable? When is cognitive theory most appropriate? When should educators take into account what has been learned from personality studies? Answers to these questions will await further research and practice and will help make accelerated learning programs more effective.

The Teaching of Creative Thinking

The teaching of creative thinking is not a new concern of teachers. They have been interested in attempting to promote it in varying degrees for a long time. The notion that creative thinking could be taught directly as a thinking skill, however, is of rather recent origin. It was previously thought to be a more or less innate aspect of artistic talent rather than a method of thinking that could be improved by training.

For some time now, there have been available a number of introspective annecdotal records about the creative process from poets, artists, and scientists. Although these introspective records have been interesting and suggestive, they have not given teachers the kind of help that they need to educate children to become more creative in their thinking.

As far back as 1926, Graham Wallas[7] made some progress in analyzing creative thinking. He divided the process into four stages: preparation, incubation, illumination, and verification.

The formulation of the creative process has been tested to some extent by asking poets whether they went through such phases in the process of creating a poem. The formulation has been verified in a rough way.[8]

Teachers can readily see examples of the four stages of creative effort in the children in the classroom. Generally speaking, however, children lack an extended period of incubation. It is difficult to determine what teachers could do to teach youngsters the intellectual process they must go through in these four stages.

Five well-known theoretical attempts to account for thinking in general and creative thinking in particular have been elaborately described by Getzels and Jackson[9] and briefly reviewed below. The first of them is formal logic, as epitomized in the syllogism. The second is in the S-R theory of association, in which connections are made between stimuli and responses through a process of trial and error. Neither logic nor associationism seem adequate to account for the phenomenon of creative thinking. A third explanation of creative thinking comes from Gestalt psychology. This explanation emphasizes the wholeness of the creative effort in contrast to the atomistic concepts of logic and associationism. According to the Gestalt psychologist, Wertheimer,[10] regrouping, reorganization, and restructuring are important ways of conceiving of the creative process. Although the Gestalt explanation is rather adequate when a problem is well defined, it does not explain adequately the process whereby one senses a problem and is driven to do something about it.

---

[7] Graham Wallas, *The Art of Thought* (New York: Harcourt, Brace & World, Inc., 1926).

[8] Catherine Patrick, "Creative Thought in Poets," *Archives of Psychology,* No. 178 (New York: Archives of Psychology, Columbia University, 1935).

[9] For further explanation of these theoretical positions, see Jacob W. Getzels and Philip W. Jackson, *Creativity and Intelligence* (New York: John Wiley & Sons, Inc., 1962), pp. 77–123.

[10] Max Wertheimer, *Productive Thinking* (New York: Harper & Row, Publishers, 1954), pp. 41–42.

We turn to a fourth theory: the psychoanalytic theory of creativity. Freud ascribed the origins of the creative process to the unconscious part of personality—that part of us of which we are unaware, the contents of which are repressed. According to Freud, the process of thinking creatively is not unlike the processes through which a neurotic person goes in trying to solve his personality problems. Later developments in psychoanalytic thinking place a greater emphasis on the preconscious processes rather than on the unconscious. The former processes are those which are rather easily made available to consciousness, such as remembering one's phone number—an item which is not constantly in one's consciousness—in contrast to the unconscious, the contents of which are not available to consciousness except under special conditions. Speculating on creative thinking as a function of the preconscious rather than of the unconscious obviously makes such thinking a process that is much more amenable to educational influences.

The fifth theoretical attempt to account for creative thinking comes from Schachtel[11] who presents a developmental-perceptual approach. What makes a person creative is his ability to be open to all his experiences in their rawness and unadornedness. The conventional person is not open to experience but reacts to the label, the familiar category, the pigeonhole into which the experience is placed.

The latter two views hold promise for formulating a systematic understanding of creative thinking because they draw on personality theory which can likely be translated into education theory and practice.[12]

Terman and Hollingworth conceived of mental ability as basically a single ability. That is, it was thought of in global terms. It was thought possible to test mental ability with a single measure and to express a person's mental ability in terms of a single score which was called the I.Q. Furthermore, the tests of mental ability tended to be loaded with verbal problems such as definitions, similarities, analogies, and verbal reasoning problems.

This global concept of mental ability, as measured with tradi-

---

[11] Ernest G. Schachtel, *Metamorphosis: On the Development of Affect Perception, Attention, and Memory* (New York: Basic Books, 1959).

[12] *Perceiving, Behaving, Becoming,* 1962 Yearbook (Washington, D.C.: Association for Supervision and Curriculum Development, 1962).

tional tests of intelligence, has not been without its critics. Some critics have focused upon the overloading of intelligence tests with verbal items, pointing out that this overloading imposes an unfair handicap upon children from low socio-economic levels of society where verbal behaviors are not as important as they are among middle and upper socio-economic level families.

Guilford[13] has also been among the critics of the single-ability concept of I.Q. He has pointed out that tests such as this tend to measure what he calls *convergent thinking.* Convergent thinking is characterized as a mental process that results in one correct and usually conventional answer. If a child, for example, is asked to spell the word *house,* the mental processes that go on within him must converge upon the correct spelling of the word. Guilford uncovered a factor in thinking which is just the opposite, which he called *divergent thinking.* Rather than converging upon one single correct answer, divergent thinking is a process that leads to many possible answers or solutions to a problem. It involves reorganizing information, discovering a number of possible solutions, and looking at the problem from a variety of points of view.

Other aspects of creative thinking are: *sensitivity to problems*— that is, ability to perceive deficiencies and discrepancies in one's environment; *ideational fluency,* the ability to produce many ideas related to the problem and to move easily from one idea to another; *originality,* the ability to produce novel solutions and answers; and *spontaneous flexibility,* a natural tendency to view a problem from many points of view, not just when asked to do so, but at any time.

An example might demonstrate difference between convergent and divergent thinking. In a conventional test of intelligence, a person may be asked to add 7 and 3. His mental processes must converge upon the correct answer: 10. A question to test divergent thinking is: Give as many uses as you can of an ordinary building brick. To this question there is no one correct answer, but a host of possible uses to which bricks can be put. The more uses one names, the more creative talent he presumably has. It can be seen that the conventional I.Q. test hardly measures the creative thinking processes of the kind described above.

---

[13] J. P. Guilford, "The Three Faces of Intellect," *American Psychologist,* Vol. XIV (August, 1959), 444-54.

Recently Getzels and Jackson have put these ideas to the test.[14] It has been found, for example, that some children when tested obtain high scores both on conventional intelligence tests and on tests of creativity. Other children were creative but rather low on conventional I.Q. tests. Conversely, still other children may score high on intelligence tests and rather low on creative thinking tests. The differences between high I.Q. children and highly creative children have been studied. The highly creative children tend to be playful with ideas; they are humorous; they do not easily accept adult standards; and they are considered by other children to have wild ideas. High I.Q. children, however, tend to be conventional, somewhat adult-oriented, and apt to fit the usual pattern of the academically-oriented child. Teachers are more favorably disposed toward the high I.Q. child than they are toward the highly creative youngster, which is understandable in view of the highly conventional nature of most classrooms.

Holland[15] studied the differences between creative and academic performance among talented adolescents. He found that high academic achievers tended to be persevering, sociable, and responsible, and to have parents who hold somewhat authoritarian values. Highly creative students, in contrast, tended to be independent, intellectual, expressive, asocial, consciously original, and with high aspirations for future achievement.

Holland confirmed a finding discovered by other researchers: that a creative performance is generally unrelated to scholastic achievement and scholastic aptitude among high talented adolescents. This finding suggests that it is desirable to rethink the concept of scholastic aptitude testing and to consider the addition of nonintellectual variables to present I.Q.-oriented testing programs.

In the typical classroom, a teacher generally requires convergent thinking from her students: to recognize, to remember, to reason, and to evaluate. Perhaps the heaviest emphasis is placed upon remembering. Great incentives are given to the children for giving *the*

---

[14] Jacob W. Getzels and Philip W. Jackson, "The Study of Giftedness: A Multidimensional Approach," *The Gifted Student*, Cooperative Research Monograph No. 2 (Washington, D.C.: U.S. Office of Education, 1960), pp. 6–11.

[15] John L. Holland, *Creative and Academic Performance Among Talented Adolescents* (Evanston, Ill.: National Merit Scholarship Corporation, 1961). Mimeographed.

correct answer to a question; they are taught that they should not be wrong.

But children should learn how to toy with ideas for in doing so, they incidentally learn much. Toying with ideas suggests to children that thinking is not a potentially dangerous activity for which one can be punished with low grades and other negative evaluations but that it is a fascinating activity with many intrinsic rewards. Children might be asked, for example, to speculate what the consequences would be if persons had three arms instead of two. They might be asked to think of what today's world might be like had Christianity and Communism risen simultaneously. Teachers can undoubtedly think up many other stimulating questions that have no single correct answer but serve as a springboard for creative thinking.[16]

It is important to recognize that the teaching of creative thinking deals not only with content but more importantly with the way content is taught. Suppose, for example, that a teacher is dealing with historical events surrounding the landing of the Pilgrims in Plymouth. What are the various ways in which a teacher might elicit divergent as well as convergent thinking? If the teacher asked, "When did the Pilgrims land in Plymouth?," she is asking a question which can be answered convergently through the process of memory. If the teacher asks, "How did the Pilgrims travel to the new world?," she is also asking primarily a convergent question. That is, there is a right answer to each question on which the pupil must converge if he is to be right. If she asks, "What might have been some of the consequences if the Pilgrims had landed in South America or Africa?," she is asking a question which will encourage divergent thinking; a number of possible solutions may be offered. Wilson,[17] suggests that creative thinking can be stimulated in the following way: By brainstorming in which as many ideas as possible are given to a related problem, judgment is ruled, freewheeling is welcomed, and quality of ideas, combinations, and improvements are sought. He also suggests that sensitivity to problems can be stimulated by asking questions such as, "What would happen if

---

[16] For further suggestions on teaching creative thinking, see Robert C. Wilson, "Creativity," *Education for the Gifted,* Fifty-Seventh Yearbook of the National Society for the Study of Education, Part II (Chicago: National Society for the Study of Education, 1958), pp. 108–26.

[17] *Ibid.,* pp. 118–26.

everyone always told the truth about everything, or if we had only three fingers?" He suggests that ideational fluency can be encouraged through brainstorming, or through activities such as listing all the uses for a newspaper, or in how many ways water can be made to do work. According to Wilson, originality can be encouraged by asking pupils to make up titles for jokes or captions for stories and redefinition ability can be enhanced by having them solve problems such as "What are all the things that might be used instead of a hammer for pounding a nail?" Such activities are interesting and stimulating devices. Creativity is probably enhanced and made more relevant, however, when it is taught in connection with the curriculum.

Creative thinking is discouraged when rigid time limits are set up in which a certain activity must be completed. Creativity is also discouraged when materials are hoarded, when errors are frowned upon, or when experimentation is viewed as wasteful. Creativity is also discouraged when children are encouraged to copy, even if their model is the work of a master.[18]

A new approach to the teaching of creative thinking and enhancement of the process of discovery is called *inquiry training.*[19] This approach to teaching is an attempt to help youngsters develop a systematic procedure for developing new knowledge to solve problems. The materials and problems are drawn primarily from the field of physics. Problems that are presented to the youngsters are primarily problems having to do with cause and effect relationships.

For example, a movie is shown in which a person holds a spatula-like instrument in the flame of a Bunsen burner. As the metal is heated, it bends downward. The operator then is shown dipping the spatula into a container of water. The spatula resumes its initial straight flat shape. The operator once more holds the spatula in the flame and this time the spatula seems to curve upward. Once more it is put into the water and straightens out.

The children are now required to discover the cause of what they

[18] J. Buzzelli, *et al.*, *Rewarding Creative Thinking* (Minneapolis: Bureau of Educational Research University of Minnesota, 1959).

[19] J. Richard Suchman, "Inquiry Training: Building Skills for Autonomous Discovery" (Urbana, Ill.: University of Illinois, 1961). Mimeographed.

saw in the movie. They are asked, "What happened, and why did it happen?"

It is possible for children, after training, to ask a series of questions whose answers reveal the fact that the metal spatula is composed of two metals fused together and that the two metals have different coefficients of expansion. Heating causes the bending. The second time, the spatula is turned over, and when it is held in the flame, it bends in the opposite direction.

CHAPTER VIII

The Role of the Teacher

Perhaps no problem is more urgently in need of solution than that of discovering characteristics of successful teachers for accelerated learning programs, recruiting such teachers, and training them for their work. Research on the problem of such characteristics is difficult to carry out. Tentative answers have been given. Until now, however, no parsimonious, unambiguous lists of characteristics of successful teachers for such programs has been forthcoming.

In one study, the following six items were judged the most important in the list of seventy-two considered of value to teachers in teaching gifted pupils:

1. The ability to foster in gifted pupils social responsibility; a desire to serve society, and a recognition of the worth of others;

2. The ability to create an environment in which gifted children participate efficiently in group discussions and in wholesome social relations;

3. The ability to develop a classroom atmosphere for gifted pupils that is conducive to mental health;

4. The ability to teach gifted children to use the problem-solving approach in learning, to apply it to independent study and research, and to evaluate their own progress;

5. A knowledge or understanding of the social and emotional problems that may be created for a gifted pupil as a result of his accelerated mental development;

6. The ability to develop a flexible, individualized, enriching curriculum which is suited to the individual gifted pupil's needs and which avoids duplicating stereotyped demands.[1]

In the study in Portland,[2] the essential characteristics on which teachers themselves were most generally in agreement were:

---

[1] Frank T. Wilson, "The Preparation of Teachers for the Education of Gifted Children," *Education for the Gifted,* Part II, Nelson B. Henry, ed., Fifty-seventh Yearbook of the National Society for the Study of Education (Chicago: University of Chicago Press, 1958), p. 364.

[2] Robert C. Wilson, *The Gifted Child in Portland* (Portland, Ore.: Portland Public Schools, 1959), pp. 107–108.

1. Greater knowledge of the subject;
2. Ability and willingness to encourage questions and independent study;
3. Willingness to work harder;
4. Respect for and the interest in gifted children.

Teachers felt that the greatest deficiencies in meeting the needs of the gifted student were lack of sufficient background in subject matter and lack of time to review. These teachers requested workshops in which they could learn more about the subject they were teaching and how to project the material effectively.

The Multiple Roles of the Teacher

The teacher plays an important role in identifying gifted pupils in his classroom. Systematic efforts need to be made to insure the training and motivation of teachers to accomplish this task. Efforts also need to be extended toward systematically including the teacher's observations in the procedures for identifying the gifted.

The teacher's most important role, of course, is that of instructor. In this role, she needs to understand and to apply broadly the principles of learning discussed in the previous section. The teacher can review her teaching methods in the light of these principles. The teacher needs also to take seriously the matter of individualizing instruction. This can be done in every assignment or project given to the children. Whether the project is arithmetic or creative writing, research or painting, all gifted students will not be able to cope with it in the same way. Teachers need to recognize this and to allow flexibility within every assignment.

Perhaps the most important quality, particularly in secondary schools, is mastery of the subject to be taught. Knowing the material, however, does not mean that the teacher must convey it in the lecture method. Recognizing that the students need to be active in the process, the teacher should provide opportunities for them to discover the new knowledge themselves and guide them in the process of learning. Utilization of a variety of resources, audiovisual aids, and library and laboratory facilities is part of the teacher's responsibility.

In many respects, the teacher also plays the role of administrator. She serves as an advisor to programs that are being planned and gives approval to them before they go into effect. The teacher also plays an important role in evaluating the program and communicating it to others. In high school, she often serves as a department head and has the general responsibility of supervising the teaching programs within her department. She also has the responsibility of setting up departmental accelerated learning programs and of planning the curriculum for the gifted students.

One of the very important roles a teacher plays is that of formal or informal counselor to the gifted pupils. As we shall see, gifted, underachieving students sometimes need an adult with whom they can identify and after whom they can model their lives. Teachers should understand this and should provide for those who need it. A teacher's informal counseling role involves showing warmth and interest in students as persons. On the more formal side, teachers can help gifted students with vocational and academic choices. The teacher can also act as a guide and counselor to the parents of gifted pupils, helping them to perceive the value of providing the maximum amount of education that their child's ability warrents.

Unanswered questions. Most of the suggestions about teachers of the gifted are too general and platitudinous. Specific questions about teachers need to be asked and answered. Below is a suggestive list of questions:[3]

1. Are the requirements for teaching the gifted at the elementary level different from those for teaching at the secondary level?
2. What level of intelligence does a teacher of the gifted need?
3. What experiences of working with children are necessary? Can experience substitute for intelligence? If so, under what conditions?
4. What type of training and what areas are most suitable preparation for teaching in accelerated learning programs?
5. What personality or character traits disqualify a teacher for teaching the gifted?
6. What are some acceptable criteria of successful teaching of the gifted?

Gallagher suggests the following pattern of development of training programs for teachers of the gifted.[4]

---

[3] James J. Gallagher, *Analysis of Research on the Education of Gifted Children* (Springfield, Ill.: Office of the Superintendent of Public Instruction, 1960), p. 115.
[4] *Ibid.*, p. 123.

1. A survey course in the general areas of exceptional children;
2. A course on the psychological and educational problems involved in teaching of the gifted;
3. Workshops to retrain teachers and to help them design methods to be used in their own schools;
4. Development of methods courses and practice teaching to be integrated into the regular teaching training sequence;
5. Advanced courses to consider theoretical and research problems.

Motivation and Underachievement

An extremely important problem relative to teaching in accelerated learning programs is the problem of motivation and underachievement. Underachievers may be defined generally as children who are not achieving at the level that they apparently could, judging from their aptitude test scores.[5]

Let us paint a composite portrait of the underachiever.[6] This portrait does not fit any one given child but is drawn from a wide variety of studies of many underachieving children. Since the underachiever is more likely to be a boy than a girl, let us call him Sam.

Sam is likely to come from a cultural background whose values are at odds with the values upon which the school is based, such as getting ahead, independence and hard work, and attaining high educational goals. Sam is more likely to value such things as keeping out of trouble, being a he-man, being smart, and finding excitement and freedom.[7] Sam's father, for example, may tell him that hauling junk is a better way to make a living than teaching is, so why listen to the teacher? Sam's friends may ridicule him or rough him up if he gets good grades.

Sam's parents are likely to have a lower educational level than families that produce high-achieving children. They are also less likely to be active in church organizations or in other community activities.

It is likely to be a disrupted family that produces a Sam. The

---

[5] John C. Gowan, "Dynamics of the Underachievement of Gifted Students," *Exceptional Children,* Vol. 24 (November, 1957), 98.

[6] For a review of research findings, from which this portrait is obtained, see John C. Gowan, "Factors of Achievement in High School and College," *Journal of Counseling Psychology,* Vol. 7 (1960), 91–95.

[7] William C. Kvarceus and Walter B. Miller, *Delinquent Behavior Culture and the Individual* (Washington, D.C.: National Education Association, 1959), pp. 64–68.

father will probably be missing from the family through desertion, separation, divorce, or death.

Sam is likely to have poor relationships with his parents, particularly his father. Boys and girls who achieve well in school name their father as the greatest influence in their lives. This is not the case with Sam. He is more likely to name someone outside of the family—a friend or a relative—if he names anyone at all. Sam is likely to have an authoritarian mother. Mothers of low-achieving girls, however, are likely to be too relaxed and even negligent. High-achieving girls seem to prosper under close supervision and control; high-achieving boys seem to need greater freedom from their mothers.

The parents, especially the father, of children such as Sam show only a limited involvement in the lives of their children. The father, particularly, does not give Sam a model to follow; he does not train him in independence. Such fathers are not interested in school projects or in children's academic progress. On the other hand, some parents put undue pressure upon their children. As a result, children may reject their parents' values completely. Lack of emphasis on verbal expression, few opportunities for imaginative activities in the home, and disagreement over vocational plans contribute to Sam's underachievement.

Sam's relationship with children of his own age is generally rather poor. Sam fails to assume responsibility for group living and for carrying out his part of social relationships. Sometimes he may even show psychopathic trends.

Sam tends to seek and find other children who are also rebellious, restless, angry, or listless. With such groups he often engages in activities that violate adult norms, particular at high school level. Sam may have a brush or two with the law. He is likely to see the world as hostile and unfriendly.

Sam's relationships with other adults are often as poor, if not poorer, than his relationship with his parents—especially if the adults are authority figures. Sam may try anything from passive resistance and boredom to restlessness, impulsiveness, and open rebellion.

A teacher may see Sam as a very difficult person to have in the room. He does not respond as other children do to measures that teachers use to motivate him. He cannot be shamed, intrigued, threatened, or exhorted into learning and achieving.

Actually, both achievement and failure may be threatening to Sam. If he tries and fails, he opens old painful wounds that have been opened and hurt many times before. If he tries and succeeds he has to re-examine and change his concept of himself, for, he often conceives of himself as a failure. Changing one's self-concept is difficult, as we have seen earlier. Rather than face this doubly difficult prospect, Sam would rather adopt a pose of boredom and detachment. His morale deteriorates and his discouragement compounds itself.

In the early stages of underachievement, Sam might simply be a nuisance to a teacher: excessively restless and unduly boisterous. Later this restlessness may turn into either passive resistance in which he gives the appearance of being defeated or bored; or if his internal control system is weak he may increasingly give vent to his hostile and rebellious feelings. Emotional unhappiness accompanies underachievement. Sam is likely to be sullen and smolderingly hostile. He may develop defense mechanisms, however, to cover his hostility and unhappiness: passive resistance, laziness, boredom.

It is important to note, however, that there are many exceptions to the above portrait. That is, some high-achieving children come from families that have all the characteristics of families that produce underachievers. On the other hand, some underachievers come from families where achievement is rewarded. Not all of the factors productive of underachievers have yet been identified. There are evidently subtle patterns of forces that operate in some children's lives that do not operate in others.

If Sam's talent is to be lost anywhere in the school system, it will probably be lost in the primary grades, particularly if he fails to learn to read well. Reading is an indispensable skill for achievement in school. Failure to develop it is an almost insurmountable handicap.

A second hazardous point for Sam will occur around the ninth grade when he is between sixteen and eighteen. A number of boys and girls drop out of school at this age. A recent study indicates that about 7 per cent of even the ablest 25 per cent of youth do not finish high school.[8] Another hazardous point is at the completion of high school: 37 per cent of youth in the top quarter in ability

---

[8] Robert F. DeHaan and Robert J. Havighurst, *Educating Gifted Children* (Chicago: University of Chicago Press, 1961), p. 34.

do not enter college. Another 13 per cent of the ablest quarter enter college but are not graduated.[9] Only 43 per cent of the upper 25 per cent are actually graduated from college.

There are still other obstacles to the completion of Sam's education. If he is a Negro or if he comes from a rural area, the chances are greater that he will not get all the education that he needs for the full realization of his talent. And finally, girls are less likely to utilize their full abilities than are boys.

Girls are often overlooked as underachievers because they seem to conform so well and achieve well by school standards. Underachievement in girls seems more a matter of lack of goals and academic aspirations. Girls who would go on to college often prefer to get married. Their motivation is not toward high development of their academic ability or other talent.

How teachers may inadvertently foster underachievement. Consider the case of the kindergarten teacher who was preparing the children for their reading readiness exercises. The children were seated in front of her and she had just finished showing them what to do with a large demonstration chart of the page on which they were to work. The teacher was particularly concerned with the youngsters who seemed to be confused and puzzled about what they were supposed to do. She failed to see that two boys and a girl already knew what to do and were impatient to get underway. The teacher repeated the instructions, however, for the benefit of the slower children. When it appeared that everyone knew what to do, she told the children to get out their books and marking pencils. Then she once again explained the task to the children who had their books open. Finally, she permitted them to begin working.

A strange thing happened. The three children who had been ready to start after the first explanation now began, one by one, to raise their hands to ask whether or not they were doing the work correctly. In doing so, they confirmed a rather superficial opinion held by the teacher: that even gifted children need to have the lesson explained more often. She little realized that she had generated in them so much anxiety to be correct that they felt compelled to get her approval on everything they did. Apparently girls can conform to such overcontrol better than boys can. Very likely the two boys

---

[9] *Ibid.*, p. 34.

would eventually rebel against such treatment if it were continued.

The deleterious effects of overlearning were described in the experiment (see Chapter I) in which the subjects were forced to repeat a monotonous skill until they were satiated. Eventually they refused altogether to continue the procedure.

A second way in which the schools may foster underachievement, paradoxically, is by overemphasizing academic achievement. It seems probable that for a given skill or content area in which high achievement is expected, a certain number of children will be found who are unable to translate their ability into achievement. If high achievement in art, for example, were to be emphasized, no doubt some children highly endowed with artistic talent would achieve poorly. The very fact of emphasizing achievement seems to arouse anxiety in some children to the point at which they cannot perform well.

Furthermore, by emphasizing academic achievement, a relatively narrow band in the total possible spectrum of human achievement, the schools probably raise a handicap for some children.

A third way educators sometimes produce underachievement is by failure to attend to the social and personal aspects of learning. The school and classroom are social settings, and achievement in them is a complex process. It has been found in one study, for example, that underachievers can obtain scores comparable to high achievers on objective achievement tests.[10] One might readily suspect that the underachievers are actually profiting from school in spite of their low grades. The reason that they may not perform as well in the classroom situation as they do on an objective test is that achievement in the classroom is much more difficult. It involves interacting with a teacher who may symbolize undesirable authority to the child. The child is also pitted against other children who may come from more culturally favored backgrounds and whom the underachiever may resent. Even when the situation is not a competitive one but a cooperative one, such underachievers find it hard to relate to other children. The grades that teachers give the children somehow reflect children's achievement as it occurs in such a complex social situation. Furthermore, the demands in school are often for a conforming type of response, and in some cases teachers

---

10 Miriam L. Goldberg, *et al.*, "A Three-Year Experimental Program at DeWitt Clinton High School to Help Bright Underchievers," *High Points* (January, 1959).

actively arouse tension and even anxiety in children. It takes a strong ego on the part of a child to withstand such anxiety and turn it to productive use. Some children who have not had the requisite training at home in postponing immediate gratifications and withstanding pain will withdraw from the situation or rebel against it and fail to achieve in it.

In some respects, the schools may extend an undesirable pattern of interpersonal relationships in the family, particularly for boys. There are very few men teachers at the elementary school level to provide a model of values with which boys can identify. In the first three or four grades, the boy is confronted with many women who are in a position of authority over him. These relationships compound the problems of underachieving boys.

Adolescent society and underachievement. Educators need to recognize that there is a more or less distinct adolescent society to be found in any secondary school.[11] In some schools, the adolescent society is more distinct than in others but it does exist everywhere. Educators who are concerned about underachievement need to include the adolescent world in their considerations. The adolescent's values impinge upon the educational program and make a difference in his achievement. That is, if the friends of a given gifted student do not value achievement, he is not likely to value it either.

Although the adolescent society is still oriented largely toward the adult world, the immediate day-by-day rewards for teenagers come from within the adolescent world. Adults are often uninformed about the effect that the adolescent world has on students, and are sometimes surprised at the apathy or resistance of students to what appear to adults to be attractive educational programs.

Coleman reports the relationship between grades, I.Q., and social rank in the adolescent world. He shows that the relationship between grades and I.Q. depends to a great extent upon what kinds of activities are most highly rewarded in the adolescent world. If adolescents value scholastic achievement, a close relationship will exist between grades and academic ability; if they do not value academic achievement, the correlation between grades and academic ability will be low.

In high schools that serve predominantly white-collar communi-

11 James S. Coleman, *Social Climates in High Schools,* Cooperative Research Monograph No. 4 (Washington, D.C.: U.S. Office of Education, 1961).

ties, boys attempt to achieve high grades. Boys find that high grades are necessary for them to enter college. At the same time, the adolescent social world draws the girl away from high scholastic achievement and orients her toward achievement in extracurricular activities. Contemporary middle-class boys admire and seek active, successful girls. They are not interested in one who is still conforming to the adult standards by being concerned with getting good grades in her studies. The boys, who are trying to break away from adult controls, want a girl who is a partner in liberation and not one who is still acquiescing to controls that applied during her childhood.

In schools that serve working-class communities, the boys tend to shun high grades and the girls attempt to achieve them.

In schools where athletic and social activities rather than academic achievement are highly rewarded, the brightest boys will go out for athletics and social achievement. The adolescent society will tend to undercut intellectual achievement. In such schools, boys with lesser ability will get the top grades and, in a real sense, the brightest students will be underachievers. Such underachievement is not a matter of personal maladjustment but, rather, a matter of adolescent values. Thus, it is relatively futile for teachers to expect high academic achievement and good grades from bright students if these are not valued highly by the adolescent culture.

What teachers can do about underachievement.   In some cases teachers can do very little about underachievement. The problem of a given child may be a deep-seated one caused by profound family disturbances over which educators have no control. Perhaps the best procedure for the teacher to follow in such cases is to refer the child and parents for counseling and therapy.

Available research, however, points to the necessity of an early attack on the problem of underachievement. The place to develop achievement drive is in the elementary school. When children become adolescents, it is extremely difficult to change their patterns.

The experiment performed at DeWitt Clinton High School in New York City illustrates vividly the need to change motivational patterns before the high school years.[12] It was found that in the first year of the study when the pupils were in the tenth grade they began to make some progress toward achievement under the teaching of

---

[12] Miriam Goldberg, *op. cit.*

a man who was flexible as well as academically demanding. He also emphasized the group aspects of learning and worked hard to make the group an important source of stability in the lives of the students. In the second year of the study, however, a change in teachers occurred, and the group was given a demanding but inflexible woman teacher. Gradually the group disentegrated until, by the end of the second year, most of the pupils had fallen back into their old pattern of underachievement. The experiment was discontinued shortly thereafter.

Below are suggestions that teachers can follow to increase motivation and thereby reduce underachievement.

One is to reduce anxiety about being wrong. Too often classroom discussion is conducted in such a way that having the one right answer is more important than having a number of answers or having creative answers.

Young people need big ideas. They respond to a challenge of a big idea and ideal. If a teacher structures his course so that time is provided for discussion of big problems such as the destiny of the world, problems confronting the nation, and the problems confronting the whole world, adolescents will respond and achieve.

Teachers also need to revitalize the classroom. The status of classroom activities needs to be enhanced. The classroom has often been stripped of its most highly motivating activities, which then are relegated to the realm of extracurricular activities. It may even be that in the future, a traveling classroom will be the most motivating classroom. For a study of political science or economics, for example, a semester spent in the large industrial centers and financial centers in the country may be the most challenging form of education.

A deeper understanding of the adolescent culture in its relationship to achievement is needed. Members of the stable adult culture need to help adolescents shoulder the responsibilities as well as accept the privileges of maintaining their own subculture. Teachers need to reward high achievement and show the relationship between high achievement in the adolescent society and success in the adult world.

Some of the provisions for increasing motivation lie in the province of counseling rather than in the area of accelerated learning programs. Examples of recommendations of the counseling nature are given below.

1. Make a survey of the per cent of underachievers in the school. If it runs much higher than 15 per cent, there may be problems of morale, antisocial trends, or other factors in the school which should receive special attention.

2. Since gifted underachievers are usually boys (by a ratio of 2:1), make an effort to assign counselors who are most capable of reaching them: a male counselor may often be more effective than a female counselor would be with such boys.

3. Give attention to building up the gifted underachiever in the area in which he has a real chance of outstanding success, whether this be music, athletics, or an academic subject. The real and enduring interest of some strong adult model figure with whom the young person can easily relate should be secured.

4. Be aware of the anxieties which plague boys at this period. Ignorance of sex, concern about his mediocre school record and eagerness to bring it up to college standards, and anxiety generated by a rejecting teacher are acute problems for the adolescent. The boy should know that the counselor has time for him and wants to help.

5. Try to find membership roles for the gifted underachiever in group activities that would require student leadership. Help him develop social responsibility roles.

6. Use group therapy because it helps to establish a peer group that is understanding and aids the development of friendships.[13]

Descriptions of several projects dealing with the problem of underachievement have already been given elsewhere in this monograph. The Demonstration Guidance Project (see pp. 72-73) showed what an entire school set out to do for children from a community which consistently produced underachievers. The project at DeWitt Clinton High School showed an experimental approach to motivating a group of underachievers in the secondary school.

Below are two other notable attempts to bring about higher degrees of motivation in underachieving pupils.

The Talent Preservation Project

The project was jointly conducted by the Engineering School of Columbia University and the New York City Public Schools.[14] Nearly 5000 underachievers in 39 cooperative high schools were

13 John C. Gowan, "The Underachieving Gifted Child, A Problem for Everyone," *Journal of Exceptional Children*, Vol. 21 (April, 1955), 247.

14 *Interim Report: Talent Preservation Project* (New York: New York City Board of Education, 1959).

the subjects of the study. The purpose of the study was to demonstrate what schools may do for students who require specialized help if the schools are provided with appropriate facilities. A complex formula, including various degrees of failure, was established to identify the underachievers. Personal data was collected for the entire group of participating students. These personal data, and the scholastic record of each student, were studied and the following recommendations for services were made:

1. Individual psychological examination;
2. Psychiatric interview;
3. Group therapy by psychiatric social worker;
4. Counseling in the school;
5. Tutoring groups in the school;
6. Motivational groups in the school;
7. Study skills groups in the school;
8. Remedial reading groups;
9. Individual counseling;
10. Grants-in-aid.

Substudies were conducted in different parts of the city. Some schools specialized in subject tutoring, others in psychiatric counseling, still others in motivational groups.

The report of the project states:

> The investigation has had an impact on the schools, the parents, and above all, the students themselves that may fairly be described as dramatic. . . . In an already impressive number of schools where the Project has uncovered urgent needs, techniques and procedures are being changed. Faculty assignments and student programs have been modified, the amount of interviewing has been increased, remedial courses have been added, and communication with parents has become more frequent. Teachers have intensified their personal attention to children who need emotional support and parents have offered, when Project funds were exhausted, to underwrite special services.[15]

The Superior and Talented Student Project

This project, sponsored by the North Central Association of Colleges and Secondary Schools,[16] was a research-action program, designed to assist secondary schools in identifying, guiding, and

---

[15] *Ibid.,* p. 14.
[16] "Identification," *NCA Superior and Talented Student Project, op. cit.*

motivating their superior students. Over one hundred schools throughout the country participated in this program (which ran from 1958–61) through the framework of regional accrediting associations. The primary purpose of the project was to create concern and stimulate action on the part of local schools and communities for their superior students. It is hypothesized that through interviews and intensive counseling, identified underachievers can become more aware of their abilities and come to make the proper educational and occupational choices. Conclusive results have not yet been published.

Bibliography

Abraham, W., *Common Sense About Gifted Children*. New York: Harper & Row, Publishers, 1958.

Anderson, H. H., ed., *Creativity and Its Cultivation*. New York: Harper & Row, Publishers, 1959.

Barbe, W. B. and D. E. Norris, "Special Classes for Gifted Children in Cleveland," *Exceptional Children* 21 (November, 1954), 55–57.

Barbe, W. B., "Evaluation of Special Classes for Gifted Children," *Exceptional Children*, 22 (November, 1955), 60–62.

———, "What Happens to Graduates of Special Classes for the Gifted?" *Educational Research Bulletin*, 36 (January, 1957), 13–16.

Barron, F., "The Psychology of Imagination," *Scientific American*, 199 (September, 1958), 150–70.

Bayley, Nancy and Melita Oden, "The Maintenance of Intellectual Ability in Gifted Adults," *Journal of Gerontology*, 10 (January, 1955), 91–107.

Birch, J., "Early School Admission of Mentally Advanced Children," *Exceptional Children*, 21 (December, 1954), 84–87.

Bish, C. E., *et al.*, "Discovering the Talented Students—Liaison with the High Schools," *Superior Student*, 2 (October, 1959), 15–18.

Brandwein, P. F., *The Gifted Student as a Future Scientist*. New York: Harcourt, Brace & World, Inc., 1955.

Brumbaugh, Florence and B. Roscho, *Your Gifted Child: A Guide for Parents*. New York: Holt, Rinehart and Winston, Inc., 1959.

Bryan, J. N., "The School Provides for Superior Students," *News Notes and Nuggets*, 3 (November, 1960).

Chauncey, H., "How Tests Help Us Identify the Academically Talented," *NEA Journal*, 47 (April, 1958), 230–31.

Conant, J. B., *The American High School Today*. New York: McGraw-Hill Book Co., Inc., 1959.

Cornog, W. H., *College Admission with Advanced Standing*. International Conference on Testing Problems. Princeton, N.J.: Educational Testing Service, 1955. Pp. 113–19.

Cutts, N. E. and N. Moseley, *Bright Children: A Guide for Parents*. New York: G. P. Putnam's Sons, 1953.

———, *Teaching the Bright and Gifted*. Englewood Cliffs, N.J.: Prentice-Hall, Inc., 1957.

DeHaan, Robert F. and Robert J. Havighurst, *Educating Gifted Children*, (revised and enlarged ed.). Chicago: University of Chicago Press, 1961.

Fein, L., "Learning Is Aggressive: Case Study Analysis of the Defense Against

Learning in Underachieving Gifted Children," *Gifted Child,* 2 (Spring, 1958), 34–36.

Flanagan, J. C., "The Identification, Development and Utilization of Human Talents," *Gifted Child,* 4 (Autumn, 1960), 51–54, 58.

Fliegler, L. A. and C. E. Bish, "The Gifted and Talented," *Review of Educational Research,* 29 (December, 1959), 408–50.

Freehill, M. F., *Gifted Children.* New York: The Macmillan Company, 1961.

French, J. L., ed., *Educating the Gifted: A Book of Readings.* New York: Holt, Rinehart and Winston, Inc., 1959.

Fund for the Advancement of Education, *Bridging the Gap Between School and College.* New York: Ford Foundation, 1953.

————, *They Went to College Early.* New York: Ford Foundation, 1957.

Gallagher, J. J., *The Gifted Child in the Elementary School: What Research Says to the Teacher.* No. 17. Prepared by the American Education Research Association in cooperation with the Department of Classroom Teachers. Washington, D.C.: National Education Association (February, 1959).

Gallagher, James V., *Analysis of Research on the Education of Gifted Children.* Springfield, Ill.: Office of the Superintendent of Public Instruction, 1960.

Getzels, J. W. and P. W. Jackson, "The Study of Giftedness; A Multidimensional Approach," *The Gifted Student.* U.S. Department of Health, Education, and Welfare, Office of Education, Cooperative Research Monography No. 2. Washington, D.C.: Superintendent of Documents, USGPO, 1960. Pp. 1–18.

————, *Creativity and Intelligence.* New York: John Wiley & Sons, Inc., 1962.

Ghiselin, Brewster, *The Creative Process.* Berkeley: University of California Press, 1952. (Also Mentor Pocketbook MD 132.)

Goldberg, Miriam and A. H. Passow, "A Study of Underachieving Gifted," *High Points,* 41 (January, 1959), 5–35.

Gowan, J. C., "Dynamics of the Underachievement of Gifted Students," *Exceptional Children,* 24 (November, 1957), 98–101.

————, "Factors of Achievement in High School and College." *Journal of Counseling Psychology,* 7 (Summer, 1960), 91–95.

————, *An Annotated Bibliography.* Washington, D.C.: National Education Association, 1961.

Guilford, J. P., "The Nature of Creative Thinking," *Research Bulletin of the Eastern Arts Association,* 5 (March, 1954), 5–9. Cf. *American Psychologist,* 5 (September, 1950), 444–54.

————, "Three Faces of Intellect," *American Psychologist,* 14 (August, 1959), 469–79.

Hall, Theodore, *Gifted Children: The Cleveland Story.* Tarrytown, N.Y.: World Publishing Co., 1956.

Havighurst, R. J., *et al.,* "A Community Youth Development Program." *Supplementary Educational Monographs,* No. 75. Chicago: University of Chicago Press, 1952.

——, "Survey of the Education of Gifted Children." *Supplementary Educational Monographs*. Chicago: University of Chicago Press, 1955.

Hildreth, G. H., *et al., Educating Gifted Children at Hunter College Elementary School*. New York: Harper & Row, Publishers, 1952.

Holland, J. L., *Creativity and Academic Performance Among Talented Adolescents*. Evanston, Ill.: National Merit Scholarship Corporation, 1961.

Illinois, University of, *The University Mathematics Program in High School Mathematics* (4 vols.). Urbana, Ill.: The University, Committee on School Mathematics, 1959.

Justman, J., "Academic Achievement of Intellectually Gifted Accelerants and Nonaccelerants in Junior High School," *Educating Gifted Children: A Book of Readings*, J. L. French, ed. New York: Holt, Rinehart & Winston, Inc., 1959. Pp. 480–89. Also *School Review*, 62 (March, 1954), 142–50; also *idem*, 62 (November, 1954), 469–73.

Kincaid, D. J., *Objectives of Education for Gifted Children in California Elementary Schools*, Ed.D. Thesis. Los Angeles: University of Southern California, 1955.

—— and Thelma Epley, "Cluster Grouping," *Education*, 81 (November, 1960), 136–39.

Kough, J., *Practical Programs for the Gifted*. Chicago: Science Research Associates, 1960.

Lehman, H. C., *Age and Achievement*. Princeton, N.J.: Princeton University Press, 1953.

McClelland, D. C., *et al., The Achievement Motive*. New York: Appleton-Century-Crofts, 1953.

——, *Talent and Society*. New York: D. Van Nostrand Co., Inc., 1958.

MacCurdy, R. D., "Characteristics and Backgrounds of Superior Science Students," *School Review*, 64 (February, 1956), 67–71.

Martinson, Ruth, Director, *Educational Programs for Gifted Pupils*. Sacramento, Calif.: California State Department of Education, 1961.

Meister, M., "Cooperation of Secondary Schools and Colleges in Acceleration of Gifted Students," *Journal of Educational Sociology*, 29 (January, 1956), 220–27.

Miller, Vera, "The Superior Child Enterprise," *American School Board Journal*, 134 (April, 1957), 43–46.

National Education Association, Educational Policies Commission, *Manpower and Education*. Washington, D.C.: The Association, 1956.

National Education Association, Research Division, "The Education of Gifted Children," *NEA Research Bulletin*, 35 (December, 1957), 163–69.

National Education Association, Washington, D.C. *Program Provisions for Mathematically Talented Gifted Students in Secondary School*, 1957; *Social Studies for the Academically Talented Student in the Secondary School*, 1959; *Mathematics for the Academically Talented Student in the Secondary School*, 1959; *Science for the Academically Talented Student in the Secondary School*, 1959; *Modern Foreign Languages and the*

Academically Talented Student, 1960; *English for the Academically Talented Student in the Secondary School,* 1960; *Administration: Procedures and School Practices for the Academically Talented Student in the Secondary School,* 1960; *Guidance for the Academically Talented Student,* 1961; *Research on the Academically Talented Student,* 1961; *Elementary Education and the Academically Talented Pupil,* 1961; *Art for the Academically Talented Student in the Secondary School,* 1961.

National Society for the Study of Education. *Education for the Gifted,* Fifty-Seventh Yearbook, Part II. Chicago: University of Chicago Press, 1958.

Newland, T. E., "The Gifted," *Review of Educational Research,* 23 (December, 1953), 417–31.

————, "Implications of Research in the Area of the Gifted," *Exceptional Children,* 25 (January, 1959), 195–99.

O'Shea, Harriet, Chairman, APA Division 16 Committee, "Needed Research on Gifted Children," *American Psychologist,* 9 (February, 1954), 77–78. (Cf. p. 522–24 in J. L. French, *op. cit.,* 1959.)

Passow, A. H., *et al., Planning for Talented Youth.* New York: Bureau of Publications, Teachers College, Columbia University, 1955.

————, *A Guide for Rating Provisions for the Gifted.* New York: Bureau of Publications, Teachers College, Columbia University, 1960.

Plaut, R. L., *Blueprint for Talent Searching.* New York: National Scholarship Service and Fund for Negro Students, 1957. Pamphlet.

Pressey, S. L., "Acceleration: Basic Principles and Recent Research," *Invitational Conference on Testing Problems.* Princeton, N.J.: Education Testing Service, 1954. Pp. 107–112.

Robinson, Helen M., *Promoting Maximal Reading Growth Among Able Learners.* Chicago: University of Chicago Press, 1954.

Rockefeller Foundation, *The Pursuit of Excellence, Part V.* New York: Doubleday & Co., Inc., 1958.

Roe, Anne, "A Psychological Study of Physical Scientists," *Genetic Psychology Monographs,* 43 (1951), 123–235.

Scheifele, M., *The Gifted Child in the Regular Classroom.* New York: Teachers College, Columbia University, 1953.

Shannon, D. C., "What Research Says About Acceleration," *Phi Delta Kappan,* 39 (November, 1957), 70–72.

Shaw, M. C., K. Edson, and H. M. Bell, "The Self-Concept of Bright Underachieving High School Students as Revealed by an Adjective Check List," *Personnel and Guidance Journal,* 39 (November, 1960), 193–96.

Shertzer, B., ed., *Working with Superior Students: Theories and Practices.* Chicago: Science Research Associates, 1960.

Strang, Ruth, "Guidance of the Gifted," *Personnel and Guidance Journal,* 31 (October, 1952), 26–30.

Strodtbeck, F., "The Family in Action," *Child Study,* 35 (Summer, 1958), 14–18.

Suchman, J. R., "Inquiry Training in the Elementary School," *Science Teacher,* 27:7 (November, 1960), 42–47.

Taylor, C. W., ed., *Research Conference on Identification of Creative Sci-*

entific Talent, I, II, III. Salt Lake City: University of Utah Press, 1955, 1957, 1959.

Terman, L. M., "The Discovery and Encouragement of Exceptional Talent," *American Psychologist,* 9 (June, 1954), 221–30.

———— and Melita Oden, *Genetic Studies of Genius,* Vol. V: *The Gifted Group at Mid-Life.* Stanford, Calif.: Stanford University Press, 1959.

Torrance, E. P., "Current Research on the Nature of Creative Talent," *Journal of Counseling Psychology,* 6 (1959), 309–16.

————, ed., *Talent and Education.* Minneapolis: University of Minnesota Press, 1960.

U.S. Department of Health, Education, and Welfare, Office of Education, *Guidance for the Underachiever with Superior Ability.* Washington, D.C.: Superintendent of Documents, USGPO, 1961.

White, L., "School Library and the Gifted Child," *Library Journal,* 78 (1953), 1480–83.

Williams, C. W., *The Gifted Child in Portland.* Portland, Ore.: Portland Public Schools, 1959.

Wilson, F. T., "Some Must's in Teaching Intellectually Gifted Children," *Grade Teacher,* 68 (June, 1951), 17, 67, 70.

————, "Suggestions for the Preparation of Teachers of Gifted Children," *Elementary School Journal,* 52 (November, 1951), 157–61.

Witty, P., ed., *The Gifted Child.* Boston: D. C. Heath & Company, 1951.

Wolfbein, S. L., "The Creative Manpower Shortage in the U.S." *School Review,* 65 (Spring, 1957), 27–44.

Worcester, D. A., *The Education of Children of Above-Average Mentality.* Lincoln, Neb.: University of Nebraska Press, 1955.

Yearbook of Education, *The Education of the Gifted.* London: Evans Brothers, Ltd., 1961.

Index